HOW THE STOCK EXCHANGE WORKS

second edition

by

Norman Whetnall

First edition published by Flame Books Ltd, 1979
Second edition published by Flame Books Ltd, 1981
Third edition published by Flame Books Ltd, 1983

ISBN 0 905340 07 8

Printed and bound in Great Britain by
Cox & Wyman Ltd, Reading

FOREWORD

by Nicholas Goodison chairman of the Stock Exchange

The Stock Exchange is a market, but to many people it appears to be a complex institution with its own jargon and its own unique methods of dealing. With the help of a good guide to explain these it is not difficult to understand how the market works. Having understood what we do and how we do it, people can then begin to see more clearly the vital functions which the Exchange and its members help to perform in the business world.

We must involve individual savers more with wealth-creating industry and trade. We must bring about a better understanding of the fact that all our social expenditure – schools, hospitals, roads and so on – and all our imports must be paid for by the success of our industry and trade in producing and exporting. Ownership of industry, through shareholding, is the most effective method of participation and helps bring about this understanding.

I believe that we are coming to the end of the period in which the direct holding of shares has been penalized, but there is still a lot to be done to make sure that those who commit their savings to the risk capital of industry are properly rewarded.

In this changing climate, I welcome this book. It is a comprehensive but simple guide to the market and its functions. It explains the jargon and introduces the reader to the full range of stocks and shares in which we deal. I wish it well.

CONTENTS

The Stock Exchange

The Investor

Investment Guidelines

Stock Exchange Careers

Stock Exchange Price Indices

Unlisted Securities Market

THE STOCK EXCHANGE

Many people are blinded by Stock Exchange technicalities which hide the fact that it is basically a very simple market like any other. In addition, it is too fundamental and important to be ignored or avoided – every citizen ought to understand how the Stock Exchange works even if he does not invest directly in shares, since so much of our future is bound up with what happens there.

So the people who dismiss the Stock Exchange as incomprehensible and best left to those with pots of money could not be further from the truth. The fact is that everybody in the country has a connection with the Stock Exchange in some form or another.

The child who saves 50p pocket money a week and puts it into a building society has an interest in the Stock Exchange because, apart from the building societies' main function of lending money for house buying, they invest millions of pounds through the Stock Exchange in gilt-edged securities.

By far the biggest investors in the Stock Exchange are insurance companies, so all the people who have an insurance policy have this indirect link with an interest in the Stock Exchange. Next in order of investment size are the nationalized industries' pension funds. The mineworkers' pension fund for instance has over £1,000 million and this grows by some £200 million a year. Much of this money finds its way into the stock market since any organization with a steady inflow of funds dare not leave the money lying idle. It is imperative that some way of getting it to earn interest can be found. Investing in company shares not only produces a continuing return by way of dividends, but may achieve additional profits if the companies do well and the price of the shares moves higher.

Huge trading combines such as Imperial Chemical Industries and Unilever also operate pension schemes for their thousands of employees, and money is regularly invested through the Stock Exchange to produce the needed returns. Other major investors include unit trusts, whose functions are discussed later in this book, the church and the trade unions.

Some would recoil in horror at the thought of the church being involved in the money making business, but religion like everything else needs day to day funds if it is to continue its work, spreading the message. The average trade unionist on the factory floor has little conception of his involvement with the Stock Exchange but the chances are that his pension fund has millions of pounds invested in the capitalist world.

What is a share?

When a new business is started its initial cash requirements – for premises, tools, materials, wages, etc. – usually come from the people who set it up. They (and their relatives) empty their piggy banks and the company starts life. But even if it is successful it will need ever more cash to bridge the gap between buying materials and getting payment from customers. In fact the faster the company grows the wider this gap becomes.

At first the money comes from an overdraft guaranteed

by directors, but as growth continues this becomes inadequate and banks prefer lending short term while the company's need is very long term, in fact well nigh permanent. Individuals who think the enterprise a sound proposition, often more friends and relatives, will then put money into it in return for a share of the business and its profits. So they get a slip of paper acknowledging their investment and their entitlement to a share of the profits. This is a share and this is why shareholders are called members of the company – they own it.

Once you have such a share certificate there is no reason why you should not sell it and so recover the investment. Say the chairman's aunt has put £1,000 into her favourite nephew's company, for which she received 1,000 £1 shares. The company prospers and pays handsome dividends but there comes a time when she wants her money back. The chairman has no spare money but by now local people know it is a sound proposition so somebody may even offer the aunt £1,500 for her shares.

That buyer can then sell on to someone else. The shares therefore are a realisable asset, but as things stand not easy to dispose of outside the family or the small circle of people who have heard of the company. It is also hard to set a fair price on shares which do change hands. These then are the reasons for going public – having the shares quoted on the Stock Exchange. It provides a wide market which allows supply and demand put a price on the shares; the shares are easier to deal in; and it gets the company more widely known and so makes it easier to raise additional capital.

Public quotation

The Stock Exchange is aware of its duty to protect the public from shady or unstable outfits and so scrutinizes every company wanting a public listing. The company must present a full history of its trading activities, balance sheets and other data connected with its financial stability, plus information about the directors. If the details look satisfactory the company is allowed to go public.

There are in fact seven ways of bringing a company to the stock market but the one most members of the public are likely to encounter is the offer for sale. This involves advertisements and the issue by the company of an elaborate prospectus containing a full explanation of its affairs, history, assets, plans, manufacturing operations, plus forecasts of profit and dividend trends. This is often issued through a merchant bank which advises the company on the best way to market its shares, on the timing, and on the price.

If the prospectus is well received, analysts and financial journalists like the background and prospects of the company, and the merchant bank sets the issue price low enough, the shares get a good response from private investors who rush to buy the new shares. Which is why new issues frequently go to a premium price (higher than the offer price) when they are first quoted.

The money subscribed by investors is used to fund the company's expansion plans, enabling the construction of, say, a new factory and a subsequent increase in the profitability of the company. Part of the increased profits would be passed on to shareholders in dividend payments, but most would be ploughed back into the business to ensure financial stability and to fund even more expansion. (Some 60 per cent of industrial investment is from internally generated cash.)

The Market

Back in the seventeenth century the old coffee houses around London's Royal Exchange were frequented by be-wigged, portly gentlemen who bought and sold shares in companies on the basis of mutual trust. If a buyer agreed to purchase a block of shares, he would not go back on his word even if, a day or two later, the company in which he had undertaken to invest his money announced bad tidings.

As the number of companies grew and the volume of share trading soared, the market was centralised into one building in 1773 and the Stock Exchange was born. But even to this day shares are bought and sold there on no more than a quick verbal agreement. Each party to a deal makes a note of the details, and the transaction is later cleared between their offices but the actual business is done by one person saying something like 'I'll buy 20,000 Shell at 570p.' Which is why the Stock Exchange's motto to this day is 'My Word Is My Bond'.

But in basic ways the Stock Exchange operates in much the same way as a vegetable market. Instead of offering potatoes, peas and sprouts for sale, however, it offers stocks and shares. The only real difference is that, unlike the vegetable market, where any individual can buy the items needed, the Stock Exchange requires the shopping to be done by some 4,000 elected members.

The reason for this is threefold. First it is a complicated technical procedure which could turn into chaos if any outsiders merely wandered into the market. Second, and most important, the Stock Exchange deals in people's savings, which must be protected from fraudulent or ignorant manipulation, and this can be done only by controlling the members. Third, the shares are fundamentally important to

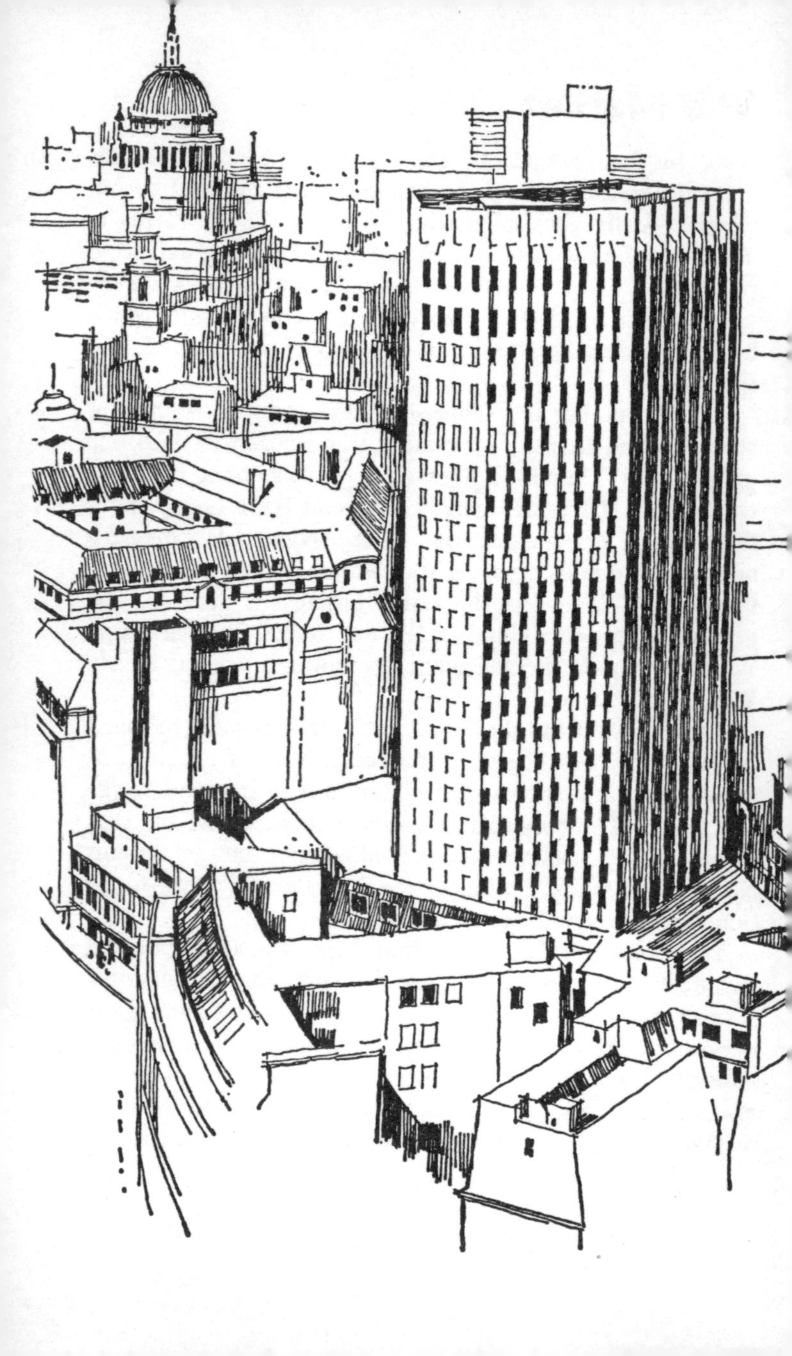

British industry, which issues them, and so the transfers have to be reasonably orderly.

'Country' units

Britain's principal stock market is in London but it is not the only place for trading shares. There are in fact six provincial stock exchanges – now known as 'country' units – which are linked to London administratively. Just as the London exchange is governed by its elected council so country units have their own controlling bodies which keep in touch with London on matters of national importance.

At last count there were 146 stockbroking firms at the country exchanges (at Belfast, Birmingham, Dublin, Glasgow, Manchester and York) against 110 in London. But some 15 of the provincial firms have established London offices. Country firms accounted for a quarter of UK stock market business, with equity turnover being greater than at many European exchanges.

There are only six jobbing firms around the country (against fourteen in London) and they transact some 40 per cent of the business with country brokers putting the rest through London jobbers either direct or via a London broker. A lot of business is done over the telephone and the motto 'My Word is My Bond' still applies.

The country units serve local investors who can maintain closer personal contact with their brokers than might be possible with more distant firms.

The gallery

It is therefore quite understandable that members of the public are not allowed on the trading floor of the London

Stock Exchange. However, good facilities exist for them to take an interest via the public gallery. The understanding of Stock Exchange affairs can be helped considerably by a visit to the public gallery, which is open from Monday to Friday between 10 a.m. and 3·15 p.m. The gallery not only provides a view of the trading floor, but a flow of helpful information. Stock Exchange guides explain the workings of the market, and visitors are shown a film about industry and its connection with the Stock Exchange. Entrance to the public gallery and the cinema is free of charge.

From the gallery itself, visitors will see what appears to be a chaotic scene on the market floor, with men and women apparently rushing around in a frenzy of business. Certainly when the market is active, the occupants are buffeted about as they try to fulfil investment orders.

The Stock Exchange Council

The Stock Exchange Council, an elected group of senior members with long experience of the market, meet every other Tuesday afternoon. Any suspect or doubtful events connected with Stock Exchange dealings are investigated by the Council and firm action taken when necessary. Perhaps in the form of a public rebuke to offenders, or even reference to the Fraud Squad of the police.

It is this strict self-regulation that gives the London Stock Exchange its reputation for integrity. As far as volume of business is concerned, the London Stock Exchange usually ranks third behind New York and Tokyo (though spurts of business change the order), but it offers the largest range and number of listed securities of any market in the world.

A 'hammering'

Probably the most dreaded word in the Stock Exchange vocabulary is 'hammering'. Fortunately the term is rarely used, since it describes the financial failure of a member firm of the Stock Exchange. The Council of the Stock Exchange imposes strict rules on market members, to protect the investing public. However, there have been occasions when a member firm has run into severe financial problems, either connected with ill-advised speculation in the market or possibly with the insolvency of a large client, who cannot pay his bills.

The Stock Exchange firm, being obliged to inform the Council of its difficulties, would immediately be investigated and if it became clear that the firm had no chance of salvation, it would be 'hammered' on the floor of the Stock Exchange.

The word 'hammered' dates back to the times when a Stock Exchange waiter (a stock market attendant or commissionaire – the term is a hangover from the coffee house ancestry) mounted his rostrum and used a wooden hammer to attract the attention of the occupants of the market. Nowadays a 'hammering' would be announced by alarm bells and a shocked hush would replace the normal clamour of dealings.

From the investor's point of view a hammering is rather less serious in financial terms. The Stock Exchange has a compensation fund for just such an emergency, and this recompenses investors conducting normal business for losses arising from the financial failure of a member firm.

Market Occupants

There are two types of member firms on the market floor, known as stockjobbers (referred to as jobbers), and stockbrokers (brokers). Like the stallholder in the vegetable market, the jobber has a stall (he prefers to call it a pitch) on the floor of the Stock Exchange. Hexagonal in shape, these pitches are easily recognized from the public gallery. The jobber can best be described as a wholesaler of stocks and shares and, during market hours, stands ready to deal with investment orders.

As I have already explained, the public is not allowed into the market itself, so that investment orders have to be placed through a broker, who performs the function of a professional shopper. Investors can, of course, buy and sell shares through their bank manager, but he merely instructs the bank's brokers to do the business in the Stock Exchange.

The people in jobbing and broking firms come under three headings. The members, who are the senior dealers, the authorized clerks, who are not members of the Stock Exchange, but who are permitted to deal on behalf of clients, and the unauthorised clerks (known as 'blue buttons') , who do the donkey work checking prices, but are not actually allowed to deal. All these are readily identified by badges worn in the top pocket of the jacket, or on the lapel. Nobody is allowed on the floor of the Stock Exchange unless he or she is wearing a badge. This is partly for security reasons, but is also an aid to the jobbers, who can readily see on the badge the name of the firm with which they are dealing.

There is a tradition that if an unauthorized person strayed on to the trading floor somebody would shout 'fourteen hundred' (at one time there were 1,399 members) to indicate the presence of a stranger. The interloper would then be literally thrown out on to the street, sometimes minus his trousers. Diminished boisterousness and better security in recent years have meant this has not happened for a very long time.

Jobbers

The operation of the London Stock Exchange is unique. On Wall Street, for instance, there are only stockbrokers, whose job it is to 'marry' buying and selling orders from investors. In other words, if an American broker wishes to sell shares on behalf of his client, he has to search around for a willing buyer of those shares, though there are also specialist 'market makers'. When the Wall Street market is under heavy pressure and investors want to sell their shares, the stockbroker who receives the 'sell' order would go into the market only to find that, because of the downward trend and general nervousness, he might not find a buyer for the shares. This could go on for days, and the prospective seller of the shares could see the value of his holding shrink quite rapidly.

The London Stock Exchange is different, in having the jobbing system, which enables the stockbroker to sell shares immediately on receipt of the order from his client. The jobber, therefore, provides a safety valve for the investor, by always being prepared, except in very exceptional circumstances, to buy any shares which come on offer.

Needless to say, the jobber has to protect himself to the best of his ability, and on a bad day in the market he would offer a low price for the shares in question. However, the broker would at least be able to sell the shares immediately.

In completing the transaction, the jobber has bought shares in the hope that he can pass them on to a new buyer, but has, in fact taken the shares 'on his book' (i.e. he stores them) without any certainty of a sale in the near future.

Why does the jobber take this risk? Sometimes, of course,

he loses money on the deal. But his is basically a 'swings and roundabouts' business. If the market falls afresh after he has bought the shares from the broker, the jobber will lose money, but if the market stages a recovery, he will be able to pass on the shares at a higher price.

In effect, the jobber 'makes the market' by carrying often large amounts of stock on his books. Apart from the resources of his own business, the jobber will often seek backing from his banker to finance his day-to-day holdings of shares.

To finance this risky business the jobber offers a spread of prices similar to the banks dealing in foreign exchange. In other words he has one price for buying and another for selling shares, and this is called the 'spread' or the 'jobber's turn'.

Brokers

Fortunately for the stockbroker, he runs none of the risks involved in the jobbing business. The stockbroker merely acts as an agent for his clients, and in completing investment buying and selling orders, receives a commission for his trouble. The broker also acts as an investment adviser to his clients, often providing statistical material for study, and maintaining an information service to larger investors. The broker will spend a lot of time, and money, on the telephone advising his clients of latest market trends and suggesting new investment tactics.

The broker, however, has other strings to his bow and one of these is acting for a company. Most public companies have their own firms of stockbrokers, who perhaps were initially involved in bringing the company to the market, or arranging capital raising operations, such as 'rights' issues (more about that later). The broker also finds himself as a 'shoulder to cry on', and as a general advisory service the timing for new cash-raising operations and other aspects of finance.

Dealing

When a stockbroker receives an order from a client to buy say 1,000 shares in our mythical XYZ Company, he moves into the market to check prices by going to the jobbers dealing in those shares – jobbers do not all deal in all shares but tend to specialize in broad areas or industries. Since jobbers compete for business, the broker might get a better price from one than another so it is worth while shopping around.

So a broker goes to a jobber's stand and says 'What are XYZ?', and since this has not revealed whether he wants to buy or sell the jobber quotes two prices. He might respond '99p to 101p' offering to buy at the lower and sell at the higher price. Another jobber in the same shares might suggest 98p to 100p, perhaps because he already had some shares 'on his book' (had already bought some on his own behalf) and was keen to sell so that he could square his books – or 'close his position' as the Stock Exchange jargon has it. If the broker found that 100p was the lowest selling price in the market (in smallish companies there are unlikely to be more than two jobbers dealing), he will say 'Buy 1,000 shares in XYZ Company at 100p' to which the jobber replies equally laconically 'Sell 1,000 XYZ at 100p.'

Each makes a brief note and goes on to the next business. Their clerks will later clear the deal and if there are any discrepancies, sort them out without involving the investor.

In this case just described the jobber is all right because he already had the shares the broker wanted to buy, but this is not always the case. If a broker had sold the other jobber

5,000 shares in XYZ at 99p, that jobber would not make his profit until he had sold the shares. To do so he may have to lower his prices to 98p to 100p, so although the spread is still 2p his profit is now only 1p.

What happens to prices also depends on the vagaries of market demand – the jobber needs to be sensitive to changes in supply and demand for shares as investor mood fluctuates. If sellers predominate the jobber will 'mark down' his prices until selling is deterred or some buyers are attracted by the lower prices; if demand rises so will prices, to attract shares to the jobber and so allow him to 'close his position' when he has sold shares he does not yet own.

Since the jobber, unlike the broker, is dealing with his own money, every time he buys or sells he is at risk until he has closed his position by doing a deal the other way. And yet, except for the most inactive stocks or where an order is unusually large, the jobber is always ready to do business without waiting to close his position first. If he were not prepared to take such risks he might lose business to other jobbers or even to dealers outside the Stock Exchange – though if a broker gets a better deal elsewhere he must offer the jobber the chance to match the terms.

The jobber is helped to bear the risks his trading involves by the Stock Exchange's calendar which splits the year into 'Accounts'. This lumps together a fortnight's trading into a single settlement at the end which gives a jobber more chance to match buyers and sellers in a way well nigh impossible if he were dealing on a daily or instant settlement basis.

Jobbers make their money by dealing in shares – their income derives from shares on their books appreciating in value, and from the 'jobbers turn' or difference in buying and selling prices. Brokers get their income from commission paid by investing clients. The table shows the scale of minimum charges laid down by the council of the Stock

Exchange. The 'at discretion' entries usually mean a purely nominal charge, but investors can check this with their own brokers. The broker will charge little if the client's other business is profitable to him but if the client's business is always small the broker will usually charge an economic rate for transacting the business which can result in a relatively high commission rate being charged.

MINIMUM COMMISSION RATES

Gilt-edged

For transactions under £200	at discretion
For transactions under £640	£4
For transactions over £640	
in short-dated stocks	at discretion
in stocks with more than five years to redemption	$\frac{5}{8}$% of the value (with lower rates if the value exceeds £2,000)

Debentures and Loan Stocks

For transactions under £200	at discretion
For transactions under £934	£7
For transactions over £934	$\frac{3}{4}$% of the value (with lower rates above £5,000 value)

Ordinary and Preference Shares

For transactions under £200	at discretion
For transactions under £467	£7
For transactions over £467	$1\frac{1}{2}$% of the value (with lower rates above £7,000 value)

N.B. The basic rates for gilt-edged may be a little higher if the order is passed through a Bank or other Agent.

We have today transacted the following business by order of :

A.N. INVESTOR

Joseph Sebag & Co.

Registered Office:
Bucklersbury House,
3 Queen Victoria Street, London EC4N 8DX
Reg. No. 982037-England. V.A.T. Registration No. 243 2127 01
Telegrams: Sebag London EC4N 8DX
Telephones: 01-236 5000 Telex No. 888631

Bought contract note

SECURITY 0-45820-1

IMPERIAL CHEMICAL INDUSTRIES LIMITED
ORDINARY STOCK

Date of Transaction and Tax Point: 4th JUNE 1979
Our Reference: 4219136
Your Reference

Bargain No.	Amount of Stock	Price	& Consideration*	Transfer* Stamp	Contract Stamp*	Other* Expenses	Commission Subject to V.A.T.	VAT@ 15 %	Net
660	1,000	£4-00	£4,000-00	£80-00	0-60		£60-00	£9-00	£4,149-60
TOTALS:									

SPECIMEN CONTRACT

Addressed to:

Net Cost for Settlement on 26 June 79 £4,149-60

For & on behalf of Joseph Sebag & Co.
Member of the Stock Exchange

Director

*Outside the scope of V.A.T. unless otherwise stated.
This transaction is subject to the Rules and Regulations of the Stock Exchange, including any temporary Regulations for the time being in force.

FAIRWAY & CO. LONDON

The 'Buy' contract note

The 'buy' contract note, illustrated above, is for the purchase of 1,000 shares in Imperial Chemical Industries Ltd. Showing the name of the client at the top, in this case A N Investor, the contract note shows the date of purchase as 4 June 1979, for settlement (the money to be paid to the stockbroker) on 26 June 1979.

The contract then shows the number of shares purchased (1,000), the price at which they were bought (£4) and the amount of money involved (£4,000). Then follows the various charges, starting off with the government stamp duty at 2 per cent, £80 (government and local authority bonds are exempt from stamp duty), and a contract stamp charge of 60p (this is to legalize the contract note). The next item is the stockbroker's commission, in this case £60, *or* 1·5 per cent of the cost of the shares, followed by the VAT rate (15 per cent) and the VAT cost (£9). All this adds up to a total consideration of £4,149.60, being the amount that the client will actually have to pay on the due date.

The 'Sell' contract note

For the purposes of this exercise, we will assume that Mr A N Investor has decided to limit the amount of money he has invested in stocks and shares and therefore decides to sell another investment. He instructs his stockbroker accordingly. In the event, there is a 'sell' note dated for settlement on – this latter date is the time when the stockbroker sends a cheque to his client with the proceeds of the sale. The sale of 5,000 shares is completed at £1, realizing £5,000. There is no government stamp duty payable because this tax is levied only on share buying operations. But there is another charge of 60p for the contract stamp. The stockbroker's

We have today transacted the following business by order of :

A.N. INVESTOR

Joseph Sebag & Co.

Registered Office:
Bucklersbury House,
3 Queen Victoria Street, London EC4N 8DX
Reg. No. 982037-England. V.A.T. Registration No. 243 2127 01
Telegrams: Sebag London EC4N 8DX
Telephones: 01-236 5080 Telex No. 888631

Sold contract note

Security 0-56540-2

MARKS AND SPENCER LIMITED
ORDINARY 25P SHARES

Date of Transaction and Tax Point: 28th JUNE 1979
Our Reference: 4219136
Your Reference:

Bargain No.	Amount of Stock	Price	& Consideration*	Contract Stamp*	Other * Expenses	Commission Subject to V.A.T.	VAT@ 15 %	Net
660	5,000	£1-00	£5,000-00	0-60		£75-00	£11-25	£4,913-15
TOTALS:								

SPECIMEN CONTRACT

Addressed to:

Net Proceeds for Settlement on 10th Jul 79 £4,913-15

For & on behalf of Joseph Sebag & Co.
Member of the Stock Exchange

Director

*Outside the scope of V.A.T. unless otherwise stated.
This transaction is subject to the Rules and Regulations of the Stock Exchange, including any temporary Regulations for the time being in force.

FAIRWAY & CO. LONDON

selling commission is £75, on which the VAT charge at 15 per cent amounts to £11·25, leaving a net total of £4,913.15.

If our shareholder, Mr A N Investor, made a profit on his holding of Marks and Spencer shares he will have to pay capital gains tax unless he made a loss in the same year to offset the liability.

All dealings on the Stock Exchange involve the issue of contract notes. The investor who places a buying or selling order with his stockbroker will receive a contract note giving full details of his completed order. This usually arrives by post at the client's home on the day after the order, and is firm evidence that the deal has been done. If the deal is a 'sell', he will receive his money from the broker on settlement day, i.e. 10 days after the close of the fortnightly account, while if the client has bought shares he will be required to pay on settlement day.

From a buyer's point of view, a broker's contract note is proof of ownership. He will receive his official share certificate from Imperial Chemical Industries Limited (in this case) in due course and some investors become a little worried over delays in receiving share certificates from companies whose shares they have bought. But ownership in any case dates from the actual transaction confirmed by the contract note. Large companies, with many millions of shares circulating in the wake of constant buying and selling operations, are often overwhelmed by paper work, hence an individual might have to wait some time before he receives his official share certificate.

The Account

Investment dealings are made up on 'account' basis, usually a fortnight long and three weeks over bank holidays. With the exception of British government securities, dealings in which are for immediate settlement, shares purchases have to be settled (paid for) on 'account day', 10 days after the close of the trading period. This is also called 'settlement day'.

This arrangement, another of the characteristics unique to London, provides an opportunity for a highly specialized and risky sort of share deal. A quick in-and-out operator, knowing that he does not have to pay for stock until the end of the account, may buy 1,000 shares in say XYZ Company at the start of the account for 85p (including commission) in the hope that he can sell them at a profit before the account ends.

If the market rises during the account he may be able to sell the shares at say 91p (the prices quoted in the newspapers are middle market prices half-way between the 'spread' so when the jobber quotes 90 92, the published price will be 91p). When he sells there will be no broker's commission though there is on the purchase, and if the deal is done within the account there is no stamp duty, so he makes a profit of 5p a share, or £50. Bearing in mind that he laid out no money at all, it is a quick profit at little cost, and the speculator gets a cheque for £50 from his broker on settlement day.

If the operator had misjudged the market and XYZ shares fell to 81p middle price, he would have to sell at 80p and so make a loss of 5p a share, or £50 on the whole 1,000 share transaction. On account day he would be required to send £50 to his broker to cover the loss.

He can work the system the other way as well. If the gambler feels the market is due for a sharp drop he can 'go short', i.e. sell shares he does not own. If he sells at the start of the account a parcel of shares at 60p and over the next week or so the price drops to 50p he can pick them up cheaply before delivery is due and pocket the difference.

And once again there is only one broker's commission to pay.

As on the optimistic tack the speculation can come badly adrift if the market moves substantially in the unexpected direction. It needs strong nerves, plenty of spare money, and a good market feel to operate like this so this sort of deal is strictly for professionals.

Cash and new

A speculator, who bought a parcel of shares in the hope of a rise in the Stock Market value over the period of the account may find at the end of the fortnight, the shares have not fulfilled his expectations, but he remains convinced about the short-term potential. Remember that the account buyer really has no intention of actually paying for the shares, but is merely in the market to buy and then quickly sell for a short term profit. He does not want to sell the shares at the loss, because he feels that his timing is only slightly awry, and takes the view that the following account could see his hopes realized.

He then negotiates a 'cash and new' through his stockbroker, thereby carrying-over his holding of the shares to the next account. This is often called a contango though strictly the two are different. Naturally, he has to pay for this service, another broking commission for the new business and a small sum involving the necessary deal with the jobber. To complete the 'cash and new' the broker will approach the jobber in the shares involved, and tell him the situation. Assuming the market in the shares is reasonable, the jobber will quote the normal dealing price for the shares – say, 100 to 103p – but because the business is out in the open, the jobber will go through the motions of buying the shares at 100p, but immediately sells them back to the broker, at say 101p. It will be seen, therefore, that the operation for a short-term holder comes out a little cheaper than selling the shares at the end of the account, and buying them back at the start of the new trading period.

In other words, 'cash and new' is the sale of shares for cash, and a purchase for new-time, or the next trading account. In this way, the short-term operator is buying time (another fortnight) during which his hopes for strength in the share price could be realized.

Options

One of the more sophisticated ways of operating in the Stock Exchange is by way of 'options'. There is a specialized group of dealers who make a market in options, which as the term implies, give speculators an interest in future events. There are 'call' options, 'put' options, and 'double' options, with various time limits ranging from two weeks to three months (nine months for traded options, see page 33).

Say an individual wants to buy shares in a certain company because he believes that for one reason or another the shares are likely to show notable appreciation within the next three months. This individual might not be able to afford the cost of buying and holding these shares over that period, so he takes out a 'call' option. This gives him the right to buy those shares at any time over the following three months, at a price set on the day the option was arranged. There is, of course, a charge for this service.

Take an example of shares currently standing in the market at 100p. If the investor were merely buying, say, 1,000 shares in the ordinary way he would have to pay £1,000 plus expenses, a fortnight after the deal was struck. The three month call option rate on these shares would probably be in the region of 10p each, so the option buyer is paying a premium of 10p a share, or £100 total option money plus expenses, for the right to buy the company's shares at 100p at any time over the subsequent three months option period.

Assuming that his judgment of the company is correct and that the market price of the shares advances to, say, 130p during his three-month option period, he exercises his right to buy the shares at 100p. Allowing for his option cost of 10p per share and other expenses, such as broker's commission, his net cost for the shares would probably work out at around 115p. Having exercised his option to buy the shares, he could then immediately sell in the market at 130p, thereby realizing a net profit of 15p per share, or £150 on the 1,000 shares. This represents a 50 per cent profit on his actual investment of £100 option money.

If, of course, his judgment of the market is wrong, and the shares drop below the 100p level, (the price at which he has to buy), the 'call' buyer would take no action, and his option would lapse at the end of the three months, leaving him with a loss of £100, plus expenses. His loss is limited to this figure, even if the shares of the particular company become valueless in the market.

The 'put' option operates in the same way as the 'call', except that a 'put' is taken out in anticipation of a fall in the market price of the shares concerned, during the three-month period. In other words, the investor is buying the right to sell shares at 100p, say, at some time over the next three months. If his guess is right and the shares drop to 70p during the time, he buys them in the ordinary way and then exercises his option to sell them at the price of the agreement. As before, he makes a handsome profit on his small investment. And once again, if the market does not move as he thought, the option is merely allowed to lapse and only the £100 option money, plus expenses, would be lost, which is a lot less painful than actually buying the shares and then seeing the market move against you.

'Double' options are sometimes arranged in very volatile shares when the market prices could possibly either rise sharply or fall sharply. In this case, the option buyer would pay something less than double the rate for his business. Option dealings are only for operators who have the time to keep a particularly close watch on market affairs, since the timing of these operations is crucial.

Options are sometimes used to hedge bets for investors who want to provide themselves with a safety-net under actual dealings in shares.

Traded options

The Stock Exchange has also made it possible to sell the unexpired portion of the option rather than merely to have to wait out the full term to decide whether to exercise it or not. There are standard 3, 6 and 9 month options – the period over which you have thinking time whether to trade in the shares – and right up to the final expiry time these options in some shares may be exercised.

The selling price of the option itself is determined by the price of the underlying share and on the expectations that the share price will move sufficiently to make it worth exercising the option. So an option which enables an investor to buy his chosen shares at 120p within the next two months might cost 7½p when the shares sell at 118p. But since on the face of it they would make only 2p profit for an outlay of 7½p it is clear buyers expect the price of the shares to rise further during the period of the option's life.

For each share in which options are traded there is at least one 'in the money' option (the option striking price is lower than the price of the actual share), and one 'out of the

money' option (option price is higher than the share price). With shares which fluctuate wildly this means that there may be several option prices available and the investor has to make some careful assessments of the market and the company before deciding which if any is worth venturing into.

Investing in traded options can be used as a sort of insurance against the price of shares one owns or plans to trade in, moving the wrong way. Alternatively options can be an outright gamble – it is one Stock Exchange investment which can quite easily lose the whole of its value, but if the price moves the right way a profit of several hundred per cent is possible.

Market Animals

Casual observers of Stock Exchange references to 'bulls', 'bears' and 'stags' could be forgiven for thinking that they were reading Animal Farm.

The 'bull' is the name for the stock market optimist who believes that share prices are likely to go higher, and who acts accordingly in his investment operations. The 'bear' is the market pessimist who is convinced that the market is due to go down, and who backs his judgment by selling his holdings.

Hence, rising trends are called bull markets. When prices are on the slide it is called a bear market. Nobody really knows the origin of these expressions, but there are numerous implausible theories. Bears knock people down, but bulls toss them up; 'bears' could have derived from 'bare' in having sold all stock in anticipation of a fall, and so on.

And from these come other Stock Exchange expressions. 'Running a bull position' or 'running a bear position' refer to the actions of the jobbers who try to run their business in a way which anticipates the likely trend in share prices.

When a Budget is on the way and most financial observers think that the Chancellor will cut taxes and so stimulate investment activity and strengthen share prices, a jobber will try to run his book on the bull tack. This means that he will be a willing buyer of shares before the prospective favourable event, in this case the Budget, on the view that investors will come into the market after the good news. In other words, the jobber will buy shares on his own account, risking his own money on his feeling for the future of the market. He would then hope to sell these at higher levels after the event.

On the other hand, if the jobber believes that there is disturbing news in the pipeline, say a powerful trade union is threatening industrial action which would harm the economy, he will attempt to run a bear position. In this case, he will try to sell all the shares on his books before the event and even 'go short' by selling shares that he does not currently own in the belief that share prices will fall on confirmation of the bad news and that subsequent nervous selling will enable him to square-off his 'short' position by buying in the shares at lower prices.

Of course, if he turns out to be wrong, this would be an expensive mistake. But if he is right the jobber makes an overall profit.

However, the best laid plans often go wrong, and a bear can often be caught on the wrong foot. In this event, the term 'bear squeeze' is one which appears in stock market reports.

If the industrial problem which caused the market anxiety was settled without recourse to strike action, the chances are that the stock market as a whole would breathe a sigh of relief and share prices would go higher as a result. The jobber who had 'gone short' by selling stock that he did not own would find himself in a tricky position, because the demand for shares would drive the price of the shares above the level at which he sold. In these circumstances the jobber would almost certainly decide to 'close his bear position' by bidding for the shares. If the market was in good condition, the chances are that nobody would want to sell to him. He would then have to raise the price of the shares further in order to attract sellers. In squaring-up his bear position, therefore, the jobber could find himself paying a great deal more for the shares as the buying pressure, or bear squeeze, intensified.

The third term, the 'stag', is applied to those who subscribe to a new issue in the market in the hope that the price of the shares will go higher when dealings start in the Stock

Exchange. When a new business, such as XYZ Company, comes to the market, the terms of the issue are worked out by financial advisers so that they are attractive to investors.

The company's shares are offered for sale to the public with a prospectus giving full details of the group's history and immediate prospects. Assuming the shares are offered to the public at, say, 50p each, and that the terms of the issue look so attractive as to justify a higher price when dealings start in the Stock Exchange, the 'stag', an essentially short-term operator, will apply for the maximum amount of shares.

If things go well, the shares might easily attain a price of, say, 65p during early dealings in the market, and the stag can then sell his shares for a nice short-term profit. If, of course, the start of dealings in the shares coincides with a poor day in the market, the stag could be forced to scramble out with little or no profit.

THE INVESTOR

Buying shares

What a person invests in depends on individuals' needs for safety, capital appreciation, high return, realisability of the invested cash, risk, etc. The first priority for most people is to buy their own home and then get some life assurance. After that it is sensible to lay some extra money aside for emergencies. It is only when these basics have been attended to that one can look around for investments.

There is a very wide range of choices, e.g. national savings certificates, premium bonds, building societies, local authority bonds, government securities, antiques, fine art, commodities, stamps, coins, and shares (either directly or through a unit or investment trust). Each has its advantages or it would not have continued to exist, and each suits a different need. A building society for instance is a way of saving up the deposit for a home but it is also a suitable place for small amounts of short term savings for things like holidays. Government securities are quite good for people who need to be certain about the level of income and about the safety of their investment, and are prepared to leave their money invested for a period of years if necessary. Shares are good for people prepared to take a risk in the hope of getting merely enough to offset the eroding effect of inflation on their savings. Shares carry the risk that the company issuing may run into financial problems thus cutting both dividends and the value of the shares, but on the other hand there is the prospect of sharp increases in the capital value if the company prospers, plus rising levels of dividend. In addition shares have an instantly ascertainable value, and are readily turned into cash at short notice.

If you do decide to buy shares the deal is almost invariably done on the floor of the Stock Exchange which means you need a stockbroker. The high street banks can help by directing customers' business through their own brokers. This has the advantage that it avoids the need to search for a broker but the disadvantage is that the investor does not meet the stock market professional who can give experienced advice, and most banks prefer to act on written instructions which can cause expensive delays.

A local broker can give guidance but he may have to charge additional fees for transactions if he deals through a London broker; a London broker can be larger and more remote but can often give a cheaper and more efficient range of services. Either way it can be difficult to find a broker who is prepared to deal with a small investor. But the Public Relations Department of the London Stock Exchange will supply a list of brokers doing this work – be sure to explain what you want, where the broker should be, and the sort of money in question, to help them pick the broker most likely to be able to help.

Once contact has been established, the groundwork cleared out of the way through preliminary discussions, and the criteria for investment decided, it can be enough to ring up the broker with dealing instructions. These instructions should of course specify not only the name of the company, but the amount of money to be invested and the price limits you are prepared to pay (or sell at).

The shareholder

If you decide to invest your savings in the Stock Exchange you become a shareholder. What is a shareholder? The holders of ordinary shares of an individual company are basically the owners of that company. Although the day-to-day running of the company is left to the board of elected directors, whose powers are shown in the company's articles of association, the shareholders have the right to appoint and sack the directors.

Shareholders are consulted on matters relating to a possible change in the company's business affairs and on items such as the sale of the company to a take-over bidder. In the normal course of business, the shareholders meet once a year at the company's annual general meeting, at which the directors present the full report of the year's operations for the approval of the shareholders.

If an individual shareholder is in some way dissatisfied with the way in which the company is being run, the annual general meeting presents the opportunity for him to raise his objections or ask questions. Unfortunately far too few do so.

A company can, in the event of a special or unusual development in business affairs, convene an extraordinary general meeting. A typical example of this would arise in the case of a take-over bid by or for another company. (Take-over bids are covered later in this book.) Summing-up, a shareholder in a company is a part-owner and is entitled to have his say in the running of the business. In practice, however, most shareholders are content to leave the running of the company to the directors who almost certainly have a better knowledge of what is best for the future of the group.

As a shareholder, of course, you are placing your savings in the future and, assuming that your company prospers, you will be rewarded by a rise in dividend payments and capital appreciation on the value of your savings by way of a higher share price on the Stock Exchange.

Unit and investment trusts

Investment on the Stock Exchange can be attractive for small savers but it can be difficult for people with little initial capital. Stockbrokers are reluctant to deal in tiny quantities, and the minimum costs can in any case make it uneconomic. Before the ravages of recent inflation it was not unusual for an investor to buy £100 worth of shares, but for all practical purposes the minimum now is now around £300. Even at that level the costs would make the deal relatively expensive and so financially unattractive. It is therefore for small savers that the unit trust business is useful.

A unit trust is like a savings club – it uses the savings of many individuals to invest in a large number of companies and help spread the risk for all of them. An individual buys units and that money is used for investment. So there are three advantages: it can take small amounts of money, it saves the small investor having to put all his eggs in one basket, and it provides a full-time investment management.

Minimum investment even here is usually over £150, and with some as high as £500 or even £1,000. They have professional management which makes it likely they will avoid major disasters. In recent years the average unit trust has performed a few percentage points worse than the Stock Exchange average, but this is a nearly meaningless comparison in view of the specialist international spread of unit trusts and highlights the need to pick both managing company and unit with care.

There are also investment trusts. These are different from

unit trusts in being a single company like any other, except that they have been set up specifically to invest in other companies. Investment trusts have shares which are traded on the Stock Exchange like any other, with the price dependent of the trust's investment policy. They do not have the advantage of unit trusts in the investor being able to invest small sums directly (the investor there deals directly with the management of the unit trust company and does not have to go through the Stock Exchange), but they do provide a useful way of spreading investment across a number of companies with a specialized investment team supervising the holdings.

Unit trusts have the additional advantage in being accessible to small regular savings. Thousands of people save through unit trusts by monthly payments as their way of getting into Stock Exchange investments. Both unit and investment trusts have the advantage of having their prices quoted in the newspapers, so an investor can follow the value of his holdings day by day.

Dividends are declared on unit trusts in the same way as on ordinary shares but many holders are quite happy to see the dividend ploughed back into the purchase of more units. And if the saver needs the investment money back it is very easy to sell the units.

Finding the Right Share

Some investors, particularly those new to the market scene, seem to believe that every stockbroker is endowed with a crystal ball, which is able to foretell the future to such an extent that the business of making money on the Stock Exchange is a mere formality. If only it were that easy. Needless to say, the professional man on the Stock Exchange has a great deal of valuable knowledge and experience and is able to guide the new investor round pitfalls of wild speculation. However, he is not and would not claim to be infallible.

Investment advice

Apart from the investment advice service offered by stockbrokers, the small saver has the benefit of share recommendations in the financial press. Prior to the last war, relatively few people in ordinary circumstances were interested in the Stock Exchange, but the post-war booms in share prices attracted attention to this form of outlet for small savers. Nowadays, many newspapers carry financial columns, with lists of share prices and daily comment on company results.

Newspaper 'share tips', as they are called, are offered in good faith after financial analysis, but give no guarantee to share buyers. They do their best but like stockbrokers, financial journalists do not have the benefit of a crystal ball and things can go wrong as a result of completely unforeseen circumstances, on the political or economic front.

As the writer of 'Tailpiece' in the investment columns of *The Daily Telegraph*, I have suffered from outraged readers who complained when an investment recommendation has come unstuck. The Stock Exchange is not the place for savings which are crucial to a person's solvency – there is an element of risk in every investment, and in shares the risk is greater than in some of the alternatives. Those thinking of putting their life savings into a volatile stock market should remember Mark Twain's dictum: 'There are two occasions when it is inadvisable to gamble – when you can't afford it and when you can.'

On the other hand, with the right advice, correct timing

and a bit of luck, the small saver can sometimes do very well and investment can be an intriguing hobby which is not only exciting in itself but does provide one with a much better insight into the economy of the country as a whole.

Choosing a share

When deciding to invest the small saver should of course seek professional advice but the final decision on where the money should go must be his own. To get this decision right and to be able to judge the value of the advice received will require quite a lot of preliminary work. The investor must sort out for himself what characteristics are needed in an investment – safety, high income right now, capital appreciation over the next five years, and so on. It is only after the basic decisions have been made that it is possible to choose between gilt-edged stock, building society, shares, etc., and only after this process has indicated shares that one can start looking at the sort of company that might fit the criteria. And all that requires a lot of thought, and some careful and realistic decisions.

Having decided that shares are the answer, the process of finding the right one to buy is one of elimination to narrow the choice down from the 4,500 company securites quoted on the London Stock Exchange.

First one must take the broader economic factors into account. The prospects for world trade, the economy of this country, and the rate of inflation will affect the performance of different industries to different extent, and within industries the impact will vary from company to company. In addition, labour relations (both inside companies and at their customers and suppliers) will affect performance.

This process may narrow the alternatives to one or two industries. The second step is to decide which companies in those industries meet one's criteria. This is done by examining their financial performance through the recent profit record, the potential for profits (which will probably include reading the chairman's statement of prospects in the last report and accounts), current trading position, financial strengths, asset values, the chances of the company receiving a take-over bid, and so on. This information will be gleaned from a number of sources – the factual material can be had from Companies House, analysis from newspapers and magazines, and advice from specialists such as stockbrokers.

The next important step is to evaluate the quality of corporate management. Unfortunately this is very difficult for an outsider yet it is vital since the most wonderful assets, healthy market, and strong national economy will help little if incompetent managers fritter away opportunities and aggravate labour problems. And of course good management can revitalise an apparently moribund company. Stockbrokers visit major companies and can give investors a personal assessment. Sometimes they publish reports on companies and industries but these too should be treated with caution for stockbrokers can sometimes be as blind as any other person.

The shares thrown up by this process can then be rated against the individual's original requirements: yield, price/earnings ratio, dividend cover, asset backing and so on. They must also be rated against other criteria for suitability to individual needs. These include the factors mentioned at the start, such as acceptable risk and the length of time one is prepared to lock away the investment. If an investor is interested in frequent short term switches of his holdings to profit from normal market fluctuations (and is prepared to devote the time and effort that such a strategy will necessitate) he will clearly opt for the more volatile shares. Or he may care to gamble on a company being taken over. Acceptance of longer term growth may indicate a 'recovery stock' – one that has problems which it has started solving, or is about to do so. This is a longer term prospect because once a company has fallen from favour it takes a long time to recover a stock exchange reputation. Some shareholders want safety and the comfort of solid worth even at the price of some lack of sparkle in performance, and will therefore plump for 'blue chips'.

Even when the company itself has been chosen the decision still remains of whether to buy equities (ordinary shares), preference shares, convertibles, or debentures, though many companies do not complicate the choice by issuing all of these.

Finally, one has still to take into account the temper of the Stock Exchange. In other words once the invested has been selected one has still to decide when to buy. Timing is extremely difficult to judge and stock market tradition has it that the small investor usually gets it wrong. You have to look at the current price in relation to the highs and lows of recent months, the overall state of the market, and whether the prevailing prices at the moment have already 'discounted' (adjusted the share price for) events anticipated over the next six to nine months. There are several ways of judging whether the present trend is set for some time or is liable to change but all are fallible. Charts may be able to help with this (see page 72).

Recognizing potential

Investment ideas are not only obtained from stockbrokers, or other market experts, since the man or woman in the street can often recognize investment potential provided they keep their wits about them Many women investors have made money in the stock market from ideas arising out of their day-to-day shopping habits.

Marks & Spencer, for instance, has many women shareholders on its register simply because they recognized that if they were spending money on good quality merchandise at reasonable prices, many others must be doing the same. The shopper who sees an attractive new product and foresees the day when many others would buy it as well, could do worse than study the shares of the company that makes the item.

Over twenty years ago during a cold winter I stood in my local shop waiting to buy paraffin for my old-fashioned oil heater. I noticed a new product in the corner of the shop, a convector heater, which also ran on paraffin, but was far more efficient in the distribution of heat. It was the only one left of a batch that this small shop had taken only a few days before. As a result, I wrote an investment note recommending the company's shares – my first attempt at investment advice – and was delighted when a year later, the shares of the company concerned had trebled in value on the stock market.

The point of all this is that ideas do not only come from market experts and investment analysts – a shrewd investor with his eyes open can be ahead of the market.

Blue chips

When seeking investment advice from bank managers and such like people, the small investor is likely to be recommended to stick to 'blue chips'. This was originally an American term deriving from gambling where the highest value betting chips were coloured blue. From there the term was adopted as a description of the best quality shares in the biggest companies – for example all thirty companies in the

Financial Times Ordinary Index (see page 63) are blue chips.

The point about blue chips is that they are considered the safest share investment. Being large and successful companies, their share prices are less liable to fluctuate widely, unlike more speculative investment in smaller companies, and their continued survival, progress and growth make them suitable for long-term low-risk share purchases. In other words, they are the traditional home for the proverbial widows' and orphans' investments.

Nothing in the world of business is totally safe though, as companies at one time considered large enough to be safe such as Burmah, Rolls-Royce, and British Leyland have shown.

Another characteristic of the blue chips is that they show the morale of the Stock Exchange. Imperial Chemical Industries for instance is considered a market barometer. Such is the spread of ICI's business that its shares tend to reflect the national economy – if ICI shares are firm, the chances are that the market as a whole is in good condition.

Gilt-edged market

Major institutional investors always have a large portion of their money in British government securities, known as gilt-edged to show how distinguished and safe the investment is. Government stocks are backed by the resources of the whole nation so although the price at any one time is affected by the prevailing economic circumstances the buyer is guaranteed dividend payments pretty well irrespective of what happens to the economy. If an individual company has a bad year the board may omit dividend payments, but even if the country's finances are in serious deficit interest on gilts continues to be paid.

The London gilt-edged market is the largest in the world. Its prime function is to finance government expenditure when the money raised by taxes is not enough to pay for the programmes the government has committed itself to. This difference between the government's income and expenditure is called the public sector borrowing requirement. At the end of World War Two the face value of quoted government stock totalled £14,000 million, but by 1978 this had risen to £60,000 million.

This debt is issued in the form of gilt-edged stock and has varying maturity dates (the date at which the stocks are redeemed at 'par' – face value). They range from as little as a month to 37 years, and there are also irredeemable stocks which the government will never buy back, such as the renowned War Loan 3½ per cent stock.

Each stock pays a fixed dividend to the investor and this is known as the coupon rate because on some fixed interest securities one had to detach a coupon at the bottom to get the dividend payments. There are many different coupon rates attaching to gilt-edged stock through the maturity range to reflect the level of interest rates prevailing at the time of issue. A few examples are

Stock			Price	Flat yield %	Gross redemption yield %
Treasury	9½%	1980	97⅞	9·70	11·40
Funding	5½%	1982/84	82⅜	6·67	10·16
Transport	3%	1978/88	61⅝	4·90	9·31
Gas	3%	1990/95	44⅞	6·83	10·11
Treasury	15½%	1998	109⅜	13·99	13·89
War Loan	3½%	undated	30¼	11·90	—

The prices and other data in this example are merely illustrations to show the market as it might be standing at a particular time. The stock name is usually given as shown, with the main name such as Treasury, Electric and so on, followed by the coupon and the redemption date. If there is more than one year indicated the government may redeem the stock at any time within those dates. It will redeem at the first date if that looks advantageous to the government – it can raise money on cheaper terms – otherwise and usually at the last date. So stocks standing above par (which indicates that current interest rates are lower than the stock's coupon) will probably be redeemed at the first date.

You will notice that the names are varied but the stocks are nevertheless all government securities (gilts). Names such as Electric or Transport denote the stock paid as compensation to private investors in these industries when they were nationalized. The price in the table, as in the lists printed daily in the newspapers, is the rate in pounds investors would have to pay for every £100 nominal (another name for face value) of stock. So at these prices the cost of Transport 3 per cent 1978/88 would be £61·62 to get enough stock to receive £100 at the time of redemption.

Flat yield is the actual amount received each year by the owner of the stock calculated as a percentage of that day's price. That is why it differs from the coupon rate which relates to the nominal value of the stock – the flat yield is the return you would get at that buying price. So £100 invested in War Loan when its price is 30 brings an annual return of £11·90.

The gross redemption yield combines the annual rate of interest with the capital gain or loss if the stock is held to redemption. So the redemption yield of one of these gilt-edged stocks is lower than the flat yield if it shows a capital loss if held to redemption. This is a result of its standing above par – i.e. its price is over £100 for £100 face value of stock. But the Transport 3 per cent 1978/88 has a higher redemption yield than flat yield because it will show a substantial capital gain if held to redemption. It is these discrepancies that give the gilt-edged market the flexibility for different investment strategies, which is one of its major appeals.

What stock people or institutions buy depends on their needs and tax position. Income tax ranges from zero for charities and pension funds, to 98 per cent for wealthy individuals, and capital gains tax varies from nothing to 52 per cent. Time scales also vary: discount houses, banks and building societies prefer shorter maturities, insurance companies and pension funds the longer dated stocks. Similarly, the time when an individual is likely to need his investment money again may well dictate his choice of maturities.

The attractions of the gilt-edged market are the ease of dealing, the range of choices, security, and the financial advantages the government gives its own stock. Huge sums of money can be invested and realized with ease and settlement is within 24 hours, unlike shares. There is no stamp duty on transfers, and profits are exempt from capital gains tax if the stock is held for over a year. With these advantages it is little wonder that whenever interest rate is competitive and sterling acceptable, there is a demand from overseas for gilt-edged stock.

In addition to the government using the gilts market to make good its shortfall on income, the Bank of England operates in this market to implement its monetary policy. It employs the Government Broker to do this by buying or selling gilt-edged stock at the appropriate time and so manipulate the market in such a way as to influence the decisions of investors.

One way the Bank of England influences the market is by issuing 'tap' stocks. These are gilt-edged stocks issued for subscription by the public from time to time as part of the government's fund raising, but when demand does not absorb the whole issue what remains is placed with government departments. When demand for the stocks revives they are released and come 'on tap' to investors.

Over the years the gilt-edged market has become very technical and brokers have set up computer-aided teams of specialists to advise clients. The large number of stocks sometimes creates anomalies which encourage institutions to switch their holdings. These considerations are based on relative cheapness and against the yield curve.

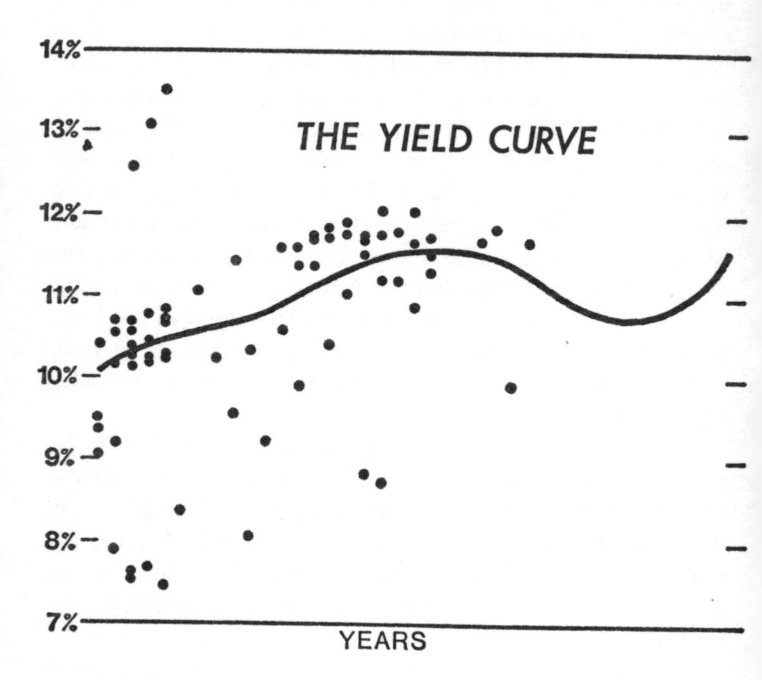

In addition much printed work is produced, together with highly technical forecasts of interest rate trends, and assessments of the economic background influencing the market.

Other fixed interest stocks

Though British government stocks represent by far and away the largest portion of the market, there are many fixed interest securities. Like gilt-edged stock the income from these does not depend on the success of the issuing organization (as would be the case with ordinary shares) since the dividend rate is fixed at the time of issue.

Such stocks are issued by local authorities, public boards, foreign and commonwealth governments, and by companies. Lots of them are quoted on the London Stock Exchange. So there are stocks such as Bristol 7¾ per cent 1979/81, London County Council 5½ per cent 1985/87 (issued before the transformation into Greater London Council), and Warwick 12½ per cent 1980. These are comparable with government stock in security so the return tends to be similar as well, since no local authority in Britain has yet failed to honour its debt obligations.

Then there are stocks issued by Australian, New Zealand, and South African governments, which are again broadly similar. There are also stocks from many other countries such as Greek 7 per cent, Iceland 6½ per cent 1983/88, Japan 4 per cent 2010, Turin 9 per cent 1991, and so on. In addition there are the bonds which were issued by governments since ousted by a regime which repudiates its predecessor's obligations. For example bonds from czarist Russia are still traded though there is little prospect of the present Russian government either paying interest or redeeming the bonds so they tend to be bought by collectors for the attractive designs. But some such long-forgotten and dishonoured bonds are sometimes repaid– the most recent example being Rumanian ones.

Finally, there is a wide range of fixed interest stock from industrial companies. The price and hence yield of these will depend on the confidence people have in the company being able to maintain payments on its capital. But for companies which remain solvent, the fixed interest security receives regular and pre-determined dividends which have a claim on the profits ahead of ordinary shares. So even in lean years the fixed interest dividend is usually maintained even if the ordinary shares receive less.

Companies issue several types of fixed interest stock including debentures, loan stocks, convertible loan stocks, and preference shares. The debenture is issued as a fairly long term borrowing and, being secured as a mortgage against the company's fixed assets, has priority. The loan stock is similar in the company having to pay dividends whether it is profitable or not – it usually comes out of reserves.

The convertible loan stock, a relative newcomer to the ranks of Stock Exchange securities, allows the holder to convert at certain times into the company's ordinary shares. If the company is doing well with soaring profits and sharply rising dividends, the holder of convertibles loan stock can switch and get the higher return on the ordinary shares.

Preference shares rank below debentures and loan stocks in the claim on the company's resources for dividend but are ahead of ordinary shares. If the company were trading at a loss the debenture and loan stock holders would still get their dividends but preference and ordinary share holders might well get nothing for perhaps two years. While the dividends on the ordinary shares would be completely lost, the holders of cumulative preference shares would get the dividend plus the arrears when the company returned to profitable trading.

Investment is not for the lazy

Investors should remember that shares are for buying and selling and should not be locked away in a bottom drawer and virtually forgotten. Of course, there have been cases where old and long forgotten share certificates have been discovered in attics and have proved of considerable value, but the wise investor is one who keeps a very close watch, not only on the shares of his particular company, but on the industry to which the company is connected. Often the shrewd observer will recognize danger signals before the general investing public and may be able to sell his shares at a good price, before a sharp reaction in the market.

To give just two simple examples, assume that the workforce of a major supplier of motor car components clashes with the management and embarks on a long and costly strike. The chances are that the car manufacturers served by the component group will have production seriously interrupted by a lack of essential parts. This will, of course, seriously damage the car maker's profit potential, so the shares of both the component group and the car manufacturers will lose ground. However, this is usually a short-term occurrence, hence the old stock market adage, 'never sell on a strike'. In this example, therefore, the investor is caught in two minds, and judgement must be made on his reading of the seriousness of the situation.

The second example, perhaps a more straightforward one, can be illustrated by the position seen in the textile industry in recent years. Home producers of textile products suffered a great deal from the import of clothing and other textile goods from abroad where producers, because of lower production costs, were able to sell goods at much lower prices than British manufacturers.

Shareholders in textile companies who could see what was

happening early in the game were able to sell the shares of British textile manufacturers before the overseas competition had time to be reflected in the company profit figures.

On the other side of the coin, subsequent Government action to curb cheap imports saw the trading pendulum swinging back in favour of the British producers, and those who had sold their textile shares and had seen the stock market price react on the import problem were able to buy back their shares at a lower level. This is what I mean by shares are for buying and selling.

Investment psychology

The small investor must learn not to be greedy. The temptation to 'hang on for a bit more' is almost irresistible to the small investor who has perhaps doubled his money in a relatively short space of time in a booming stock market. The problem is, of course, that in hanging on for a bit more, the market boom could run out of steam, and the price of the shares could fall equally swiftly.

Another old stock market adage is 'it is never wrong to take a profit'. What this basically means is that, if the investor gets to a situation where the price of his shares has rocketed beyond the levels at which the basic investment attractions, such as dividend yield, are leaving little room for further market appreciation, he should sell and be content with what he has achieved.

The proceeds of his sale can then be re-invested in another, more promising, investment where he can build on his previous success. Of course nobody can tell with certainty absolutely the right time to buy and sell individual shares, but the greedy temptation to hold on for an even higher price should be resisted. And conversely do not try to wait for the bottom of the market to buy.

Following prices

Progress of investments can be followed in the stock market pages of the financial press. The shares are listed by sectors and the sectors themselves are in alphabetical order though they start with British Funds (government securities). The extent of coverage of prices and statistical information in the newspapers is obviously determined by the type of readership, with the quality newspapers giving more data. However, the popular papers have increased their coverage of the stock market in recent years on the realization that investment is not confined to the rich.

It takes experience though to understand even the information printed on the newspapers' prices pages. So here are examples of the way this is presented in the *Financial Times* and *The Daily Telegraph*. First the *Financial Times*.

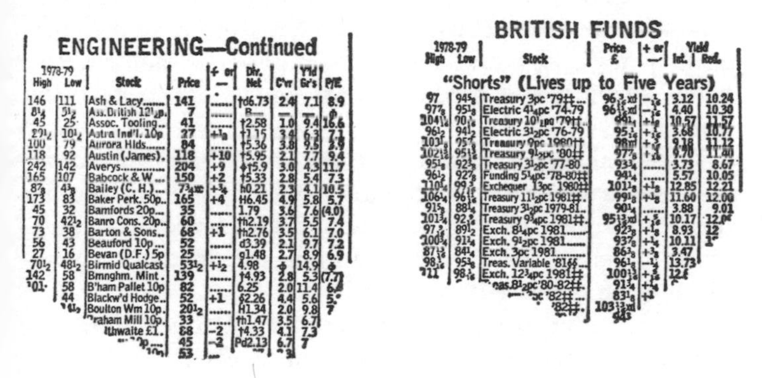

ENGINEERING—Continued

1978-79 High	Low	Stock	Price	+ or −	Div. Net	C'vr	Y'ld Gr's	P/E
146	111	Ash & Lacy	141	......	†d6.73	2.4	7.1	8.9
8¼	5½	Ass. British 12½p.	7	......	B—	—	—	ϕ
45	25	Assoc. Tooling	41	......	†2.58	1.0	9.4	16.6
29½	10½	Astra Ind'l. 10p	27	+⅛	†1.15	3.4	6.3	7.1
100	79	Aurora Hlds.	84	......	†5.36	3.8	9.5	3.9
118	92	Austin (James).	118	+10	†5.95	2.1	7.7	9.4
242	142	Averys	204	+9	ϕ†5.9	3.0	4.3	11.7
165	107	Babcock & W	150	+2	†5.33	2.8	5.4	7.3
8⅞	4⅜	Bailey (C. H.)	7¾xc	+¾	h0.21	2.3	4.1	10.5
173	83	Baker Perk. 50p	165	+4	H6.45	4.9	5.8	5.7
45	32	Bamfords 20p	35	......	1.79	3.6	7.6	(4.0)
70	42½	Banro Cons. 20p	60	......	†h2.19	3.7	5.5	7.4
73	38	Barton & Sons	68	+1	†h2.76	3.5	6.1	7.0
56	43	Beauford 10p	52	......	d3.39	2.1	9.7	7.2
27	16	Bevan (D.F.) 5p	25	......	g1.48	2.7	8.9	6.9
70½	48½	Birmid Qualcast	53½	+½	4.98	ϕ	14.9	ϕ
142	58	Bmnghm. Mint.	139	......	†4.93	2.8	5.3	(7.7)
101	58	B'ham Pallet 10p	82	......	6.25	2.0	11.4	6.[illegible]
	44	Blackw'd Hodge	52	+1	§2.26	4.4	5.6	5.[illegible]
	[illegible]	Boulton Wm 10p.	20½	......	H1.34	2.0	9.8	7
		[illegible]raham Mill 10p.	33	......	†h1.47	3.5	6.7	
		[illegible]thwaite £1.	88	−2	†4.33	4.1	7.3	
		[illegible]0p	45	−2	Pd2.13	6.7	7	
		[illegible]10p	53	—	[illegible]	[illegible]		

BRITISH FUNDS

1978-79 High	Low	Stock	Price £	+ or −	Yield Int.	Red.
		"Shorts" (Lives up to Five Years)				
97	94⅝	Treasury 3pc '79‡‡	96 3/16xd	−1/16	3.12	10.24
97⅞	95⅛	Electric 4¼pc '74-79	96 11/16xd	−1/16	4.40	10.30
104 11/16	90 1/16	Treasury 10½pc '79‡‡	99¼	+⅛	10.57	11.57
96½	94½	Electric 3½pc '76-79	95 1/16	+1/16	3.68	10.77
103⅛	95⅞	Treasury 9pc 1980‡‡	98xd	+3/16	9.18	11.12
102 15/16	95 13/16	Treasury 9½pc '80‡‡	97⅞	+1/16	9.70	11.40
95⅛	92⅜	Treasury 3½pc '77-80	93¾	......	3.73	8.67
96½	92⅞	Funding 5¼pc '78-80‡‡	94¼	......	5.57	10.05
110¼	99 3/16	Exchequer 13pc 1980‡‡	101⅛	+⅛	12.85	12.21
106¼	96 11/16	Treasury 11½pc 1981‡‡	99⅛	+⅛	11.60	12.00
91⅝	88¼	Treasury 3½pc 1979-81	90¼	......	3.88	9.01
101¾	92 9/16	Treasury 9¾pc 1981‡‡	95 13/16xd	+5/16	10.17	12.0[illegible]
97 9/16	89½	Exch. 8¼pc 1981	92⅜	+⅛	8.93	12[illegible]
100¾	91¼	Exch. 9½pc 1981	93⅞	+¼	10.11	1[illegible]
87 13/16	84¼	Exch. 3pc 1981	86⅜	+⅜	3.47	
98 1/16	95⅜	Treas. Variable '81‡‡	96⅛	−¼	13.73	
111	98 1/16	Exch. 12¾pc 1981‡‡	100 13/16	+3/16	12.[illegible]	
		[illegible]eas. 8½pc '80-82‡‡	91¾	+¼		
		[illegible]pc '82‡‡	83⅛	+1		
		[illegible]'82‡‡	103 13/16xd			
			94[illegible]			

In both the illustrations the first two columns, marked '1978–79 High Low', indicate the highest and lowest price that security reached in the period specified. During the first three months of each year the previous year's levels are also included.

In the next column, headed 'Stock', comes the name of the security. In the case of British Funds (commonly called gilts) it names the type of stock, its nominal interest and date of redemption, e.g. Treasury 10½ pc '79. The quadruple daggers after some stock indicates that these are tax free to non-residents on application. In the case of an industrial stock the list gives an abbreviated name of the corporation and if the shares are not at 25p face value, it adds what the nominal price is.

The column following gives the previous day's closing price. For gilts this is in pounds, for shares in pennies. Then comes the previous day's change + or —.

For gilts the next two columns, headed 'Yield', then show the return obtainable from each stock. The column marked 'Int' gives the return on that stock at the closing price – e.g. if an investor put £100 into Treasury 3½ per cent '77–80 at the price of 93¾, he would get a return of 3·73 per cent. If however he held it to redemption he would get a bonus which would produce a rate equivalent to 8·67 per cent.

Industrial companies list 'Div net' which gives the actual payment made by the corporation. So Averys for instance in this illustration paid 5·9p per share (the diamond indicates a bid in progress, the dagger shows that the dividend has recently been increased).

'Covr' indicates cover – the number of times more the company could have paid that level of dividend. For instance Associated Tooling has its dividend covered once which means it had sufficient profits to pay a 5·16p per share dividend but retained the rest to reinvest.

'Y'ld Gr's' is a tortured contraction of gross yield and is the equivalent to the gilts 'Int'. So £100 invested in Barton and Sons at 68p would produce a return of £6·10 (assuming the dividend remained unchanged).

'P/E' is the ratio of current price to company earnings. For an explanation of the calculation and the significance of this column see the section on Investment Figures on page 68.

BRITISH FUNDS

Short-dated (up to 5 years)

1978-79 High £	Low £	Stock	Price	+ or −
105 1/8	99 13/16	Treas. 11½% 1979	£99 15/16	..
97	94¾	Treas. 3% 1979	£96 1/16	−1/16
97⅞	93⅜	Elec. 4½% 74-79	£95 11/16	−1/16
104 11/16	90 1/16	Treas. 10½% 1979	£98 15/16	−1/16
96½	94⅛	Elec. 3½% 76-79	£95⅜	−⅛
103⅛	96⅜	Treas. 9% 1980	£96 15/16	−⅛
102 15/16	93⅜	Treas. 9½% 1980	£96 15/16	−⅛
95⅛	92⅝	Treas. 3½% 77-80	£94¼	−⅛
99¼	93¼	Fndg. 5½% 78-80	£94⅜	−1/16
110¼	100⅜	Exch. 13% 1960	£100⅜	−5/16
106¼	97⅝	Treas. 11½% 1981	£98	−⅜
91⅝	88¼	Treas. 3½% 79-81	£89¾	−⅛
101¾	94	Treas. 9¾% 1981	£94	−5/16
97 9/16	90¾	Exch. 8¼% 1981	£90¾	−7/16
100¾	92⅝	Exch. 9½% 1981	£92⅝	−⅜
87 13/16	81	Exch. 3% 1981	£85½	−1/16
97⅞	95⅜	Treas. V/R 1981	£97⅞	+1/16
111	99½	Exch. 12¾% 1981	£99½	−⅜
99⅜	89¾	Treas. 8½% 80-82	£90	+5/16
86⅝	82⅞	Treas. 3% 1982	£83⅞	−⅛
115⅞	100 1/16	Treas. 14% 1982	£102¼	−7/16
104⅛	94	Treas. V/R 1982	£96⅝	+1/16
96⅜	87¾	Treas. 8¼% 1982	£87 11/16	−¼
100¼	88⅝	Exch. 9¾% 1982	£88¾	−⅜
96 13/16	87	Exch. 8½% 1983	£87	−⅜
84¾	79 7/16	Exch. 3% 1983	£79 7/16	−⅛
114¼	96¼	Treas. 12% 1983	£96¼	−7/16
106⅝	87	Treas. 9¼% 1983	£87	−7/16
95 3/16	88	Exch. 10% 1983	£88¼	−7/16
89⅝	80¼	Fndg. 5½% 82-84	£81¼	−⅛

[illegible]m-dated (five to fifteen)

Stock	Price	+ or −
Exch. 12¼% 1985	£96¼	−¼
[illegible]eas. 8½% 84-86	£82⅞	−¼
6½% 85-87	£75⅜	−¼
[illegible]% 85-88	£76⅛*	−¼
[illegible]% 78-88	£61⅜	−¼
[illegible]86-89	£64⅛	−¼
[illegible]990	£97⅞*	−¼
[illegible]-90	£75⅞	−¼
[illegible]	£90⅛	−¼
[illegible]	£63⅜	−¼
[illegible]	[illegible]95⅜	−¼
[illegible]	[illegible]	−¼
[illegible]	[illegible]	−⅜

BUILDING & ROADS

1978-79 High	Low	Stock	Price	+ or −
43	28	Abbey Ltd....	36	..
102	76	AberdeenCons	76	..
164	138	Aberthaw Cmt	140	..
21½	13	Allied Plant..	21	..
84	59½	Armitage S...	84	+9
16	10	Bailey Ben....	15	..
129	98	Barret Devel..	102	..
32½	21½	Beechwood ...	30	..
68	52	Bett Bros.	58	..
98	58	B'ham Pallet.	80*	..
85	62	Blockleys......	71	..
303	220	Blue Circle....	272	+2
89	60	Blundell Perm	89	..
264	202	B.P.B. Indus.	252	−1
107	75	Breedon Clond	105	..
41	21	Brit. Dredging	29	..
276	24	Brown & Jack	275	..
81½	45	Brownlee	80½	+½
57	36	Bryant Hldg..	49	..
244	152	Burnett&Hllsh	244	..
43	22	CakebredR'A'	35	..
59	41	Carr John.....	59	+4
70	40	Carron	67	..
109	68	Cement Rdstn	109	..
38	27	Comben	33	..
18	16	Copson, F.....	16	..
224	122	Costain	178	..
146	138	CostainGpDfd	138	−2
53	30	Countryside ..	52	..
120	80	Crouch D......	118	−2
73	62	Crouch Group	69	..
104	84	Douglas R. M.	84	..
162	100	Downing G.H.	122	..
110	68	Erith & Co....	109	..
26	10	F.P.A. Constr.	13½	.
79	59	FairclougCn.	64	.
29	19	Feb. Internatl	28	
57	34	Federated Lnd	56½	
36	21	Finlan John..	29	
55	40	Francis G. R.	55	
21	11½	FrancisParker	18	
41	26½	French Kier..	30	
75	52	GallifordBrdly	7[illegible]	
49	34	Gleeson M. J..		
69	48	Glossop W. &J		
86	68	Gough Coop[illegible]		
31½	24½	H.A.T. Gr[illegible]		
41	22	Helical B[illegible]		
75	40½	Hewder[illegible]		
158	64	Heyw[illegible]		
93	63	Hig[illegible]		
[illegible]	68	[illegible]		

The Daily Telegraph carries similar information but has fewer columns. As can be seen from these illustrations the information is the high and low of the price attained, the name of the stock or company, the latest closing price, and the change of price during the previous trading day.

The lists published in the daily newspapers are based on the 'middle' prices quoted by the jobbers. If the dealing spread on a certain share was 98p to 102p, the price would appear as 100p in the newspapers. An investor studying the City prices list would, therefore, have to make allowance for this in buying and selling. But even then there is no guarantee that he would be able to buy and sell shares at these levels, even if he were quick off the mark at the start of dealings. Jobbers often raise or lower price levels before the opening of the day's business, particularly if there is some overnight development which could set a new trend in the stock market as a whole.

The Stock Exchange prices published in the press should be taken as only a guide to market values and the investor who wants to act quickly has only to telephone his broker, who will check the price of any individual issue, usually within a minute or two.

This method is recommended to investors who perhaps have seen favourable comment on a certain company's shares, and who are impressed enough to place a buying order. Remember that the jobber in the shares concerned has also seen the favourable comment and, likely as not, has anticipated a rise in demand for the shares by marking-up the price by a penny or two before the start of trading. Investors sometimes complain that they envisaged paying, say 100p, for the shares of a certain company, but when the contract note arrived from the broker, the price paid was 104p. It is therefore quite important either to get the broker to check the price before dealing, or to give the broker a 'limit'. The investor may be prepared to pay 102p for the shares concerned and would instruct his broker accordingly, thereby placing a buying limit of 102p. The broker would then either deal at 102p or, if the price was higher, would wait for further instructions from his client. The investor can also place sell 'limits' with his broker, who will tell the jobber that he is prepared to sell shares at a certain level. If the market price of the shares goes higher during the course of time, the jobber will then bid the broker for the shares at the selling limit. The client then obtains the price he was seeking for his shares.

'Market sentiment' is a term used by Stock Exchange commentators and readers of financial columns will often see a quote: 'sentiment was adversely affected by trans-atlantic parities'. This is merely a pompous way of saying that, because of a downward trend of share prices on Wall Street, the London stock market was nervous about prospects for the American market. In other words, 'sentiment' is a term relating to the basic feeling of the stock market at any particular time. A bearish sentiment, or pessimistic feeling, will cause the prices to drift lower, while bullish sentiment, or optimistic feeling, will find prices in a mood to move ahead.

The Stock Exchange can be affected by all sorts of political and economic events and market sentiment can change very rapidly from one mood to the other.

The investor who is divorced from day-to-day market sentiment and is not subjected to the ups and downs of market mood, is sometimes able to make clearer investment judgment simply because he is not unduly influenced by what, after all, are very short-term considerations. Jobbers and brokers on the Stock Exchange floor often admit being in a situation where 'we can't see the wood for the trees'. This means that the day's market sentiment has been so affected by events, perhaps completely unconnected with the stock market itself, that normal investment criteria are temporarily replaced by irrational feelings. An old stock market adage is 'majority opinion is often wrong', at least in the short term.

Some shrewd investors make money by doing the opposite to the majority. If all is gloom and misery on the Stock Exchange owing to short-term worries, the shrewd investor, having done his sums on a particular share favourite, will buy while others are selling, thereby taking advantage of a bargain hunting opportunity. When market sentiment takes a turn for the better, as it almost invariably does after a very dull phase, the chances are that the shares he has bought at a 'cheap' level, will appreciate in value as they take account of straightforward investment statistics rather than a generally weak overall situation in the market. The investor who takes these decisions must be fairly sophisticated in that he knows the background of the shares involved to such an extent that he is working on intrinsically sound buying principles.

The stock market is a strange place, being affected by political and economic considerations far beyond the day to day affairs of individual companies. It is also an emotional, gossipy place, given to rumours, panics and wildly mystifying fluctuations. While certain shares can look excellent value, and well worth investment money on trading grounds, the value of the shares can decline simply because the market as a whole is affected by an outside influence.

Take January 1 1975, when the market was poised to push ahead with its traditional bout of New Year optimism. Out of the blue came news of a major financial crash in the business world; that of the huge Burmah Oil Company. The repercussions of this company's failure brought a sense of panic in the stock market and share prices plummeted across the board. Such was the mood of panic that rumours were rife, casting doubts on the financial solvency of many other major British companies. In the event, small investors rushed to sell shares in perfectly sound concerns, and the overall situation was reflected in the lowest-ever prices for many shares. When the panic subsided, however, shrewd investors took advantage of what turned out to be bargain-basement values, and the brave made small fortunes as the market rebounded from a January 6 level of 146 in the Financial Times Industrial Ordinary Share Index (the leading measurement of industrial share trends) to 301·8, in the space of only seven weeks. Burmah was later restored to health and is now one of Britain's larger oil companies.

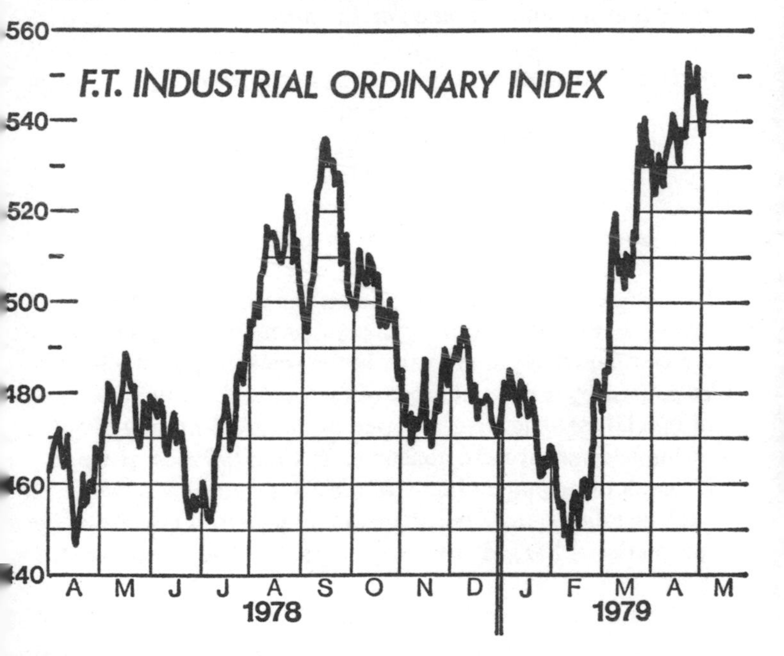

Needless to say, many small investors were shattered by this experience (some market men still say that things will never be the same again) but this emphasizes the point that there is always a risk in stockmarket investment, and that even the best investment advice available can be upset by a totally unexpected event.

In considering stock market fluctuations the investor needs a cool, calculating head to decide how substantial a change is – i.e. is it a short term movement, the first hint of a bigger alteration, or the start of a major new trend. The problem is of course not unique to stock markets but applies also to the economy at large of which share prices are a reflection. Sir Alec Cairncross, a former economic adviser to the Treasury, once summed up the dilemma:

A trend (to use the language of Gertrude Stein) is a trend is a trend.
But the question is: will it bend?
Will it alter its course
Through some unforeseen force,
And come to a premature end?

In Stock Exchange parlance this is the difference between a primary, secondary and tertiary price movement. Tertiaries are comparatively small yaws in the price graphs. These can be caused by a large number of factors such as the latest set of official statistics (e.g. the rate of inflation, money supply, unemployment trends, consumer buying, balance of trade); by news of an impending strike by a group of key workers such as miners, dockers or electricity generating staff; or by international hazards such as the prospect of a middle east war.

Secondary movements are caused by a more substantial change in general confidence. These are more subtle and take longer to become evident. They can be triggered by one of the factors causing tertiary changes, by news of budgets,

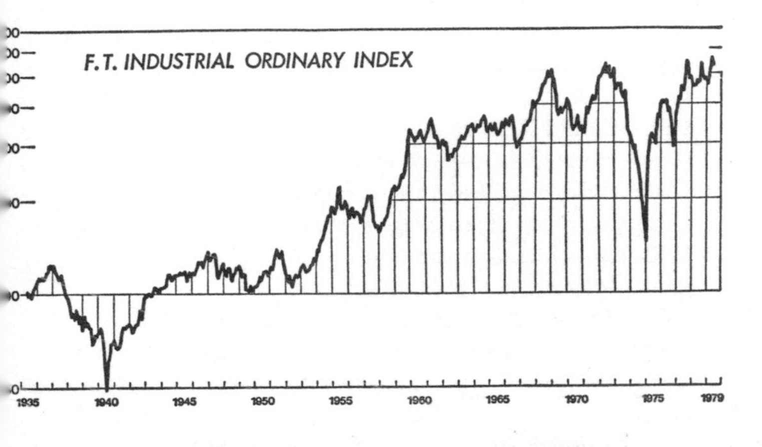

or by expectations of a general election, but more usually the alteration in market sentiment is the result of an accumulation of factors pointing in the same direction. Such secondary movements can last anything from a few weeks to several months.

The primary movement is the broad sweep of a long term trend which can be over two years long. It can be interrupted by secondary movements in the opposite direction (with tertiaries superimposed on top of the secondaries), but the overall trend continues none the less. One can tell when a primary or even secondary movement is well established – as either a bull or a bear market – by the way some news which ought to affect the market the other way is ignored, or shrugged off with small changes which are quickly corrected. So entrenched euphoria is not upset by poor results from ICI, or even one month's bad trade figures, and profound gloom is not reversed by better news.

All this is basically the language used by chartists (see page 72) but whether one follows, or even believes in the use of, charts an appreciation of the fact that changes may be temporary fluctuations or parts of major changes, is useful to an investor deciding tactics. Acting on tertiary movements can be hazardous – the change may be so quick that the decision to trade could miss it, or it may be too small to offset the costs of dealing. Assessing the power and duration of secondary movements to gauge the correct time to deal requires skill, and of course the investor who can spot a primary change can make a lot of money.

The London market has been particularly volatile and it takes strong nerves to withstand the stampedes in either direction. It is not a place for making easy money. With good advice, luck and a cool head you can invest successfully but it is not the place for any money you cannot afford to lose.

A classic example of the boom and bust swings of the market when investment activity is all one way is the Australian nickel share market, where a few years back fortunes were made and lost literally overnight. The story is worth recalling since there are lessons to be learned by the small investor.

Nickel was in very short supply in 1969 mainly as a result of a long strike at the Canadian nickel mines of International Nickel, and Falconbridge and the free market price of the metal soared from the official producers' price of £986 per ton, to over £7,500 per ton. As a result any mining company with nickel deposits came under intense scrutiny, and a name came into the stock market vocabulary which will long be remembered as an example of speculative greed. The name was Poseidon, a nickel exploration company with some obscure leases in Western Australia. The tiny township of Laverton, Western Australia, was put on the world map overnight by the Poseidon nickel strike which produced scenes making the American gold rushes look like a relatively quiet Saturday morning in a Tesco food store.

The township was inundated with prospectors, farmers, businessmen, and clerks who caught the nickel fever. The tracks of bushland surrounding Laverton were soon swarming with professional and non-professional prospectors pegging claims to what they hoped would reveal substantial nickel deposits. Around 50 mining companies were also busy staking claims and, when the news got through to the Australian and London stock markets, share prices went berserk. In Australia, everybody with money to spare became a speculator on the stock market. Many made a great deal of money by selling shares at inflated levels, but many more ended up poorer and wiser.

The Sunday Telegraph City pages of December 28 1969, carried a feature article headlined 'The Nickel Craze Is Out of Hand', and suggested that nickel mania reflected in the stock market boom would blow its top as disastrously as the Canadian market in the late fifties. The market fever on Christmas Eve is illustrated by the shares of North Flinders, which opened at £3·50 and closed at £10; when dealings resumed after the Christmas holiday, the price of North Flinders immediately dropped to £5 and went on falling.

North Flinders was a one-day phenomenon. Poseidon shares showed even crazier movements. From September 1969 to February 1970 the price soared from 30p to £132 but then declined to 75p in October 1976 when a receiver was appointed. Poseidon is now back in business as a well-regarded gold investment.

Probably the overall market situation, and a sad commentary on the dangers of speculation, were adequately covered by a small poem written by *The Sunday Telegraph*

City journalists, at the time of the boom in North Flinders shares. It ran:

Little Polly Flinders
Scratched among the cinders
Prospecting for nickel and gold,
Investors being fickle,
Thought that she'd struck nickel
And bought when they ought to have sold.

Investment figures

Small savers in the Post Office, building societies and bank deposit accounts have little difficulty in understanding the value of their savings, because the rates of interest paid are well known and easy to grasp. When a small saver looks at the Stock Exchange as a potential home for his money, he is often confused by terms such as 'dividend yield', 'dividend cover', and 'price/earnings ratio'. These formidable-looking terms are well worth learning, because the small saver can then make his own judgment on the attractions or otherwise of a company.

Although an investor can rely on his broker to produce investment ideas related to income needs, etc, he should take the trouble to understand the meaning of the investment statistics relating to shares of any company in which he is interested.

A 5 per cent interest rate on a deposit account in a bank will bring an annual income of £5 for every £100 invested. In exactly the same way, a dividend yield of 8·5 per cent will bring an income, before tax, of £8·50 for every £100 invested in the particular share. This has nothing to do with the face value (or 'par value') of the share, nor with the price an investor may have paid for them sometime in the past. It is a simple expression of how much £100 invested at that day's price in those shares would yield at the current rate of dividend.

For shares standing at 50p, investor would get 200 of them for his £100. If the company is paying a dividend of 10p a share this year, the investor would get £20 – 20 per cent. This return is known as the dividend yield and is one of the vital statistics taken into account when selecting an investment prospect.

'Dividend cover' gives the investor a guide to the individual company's financial background. If after all expenses a company ends up with profits of £300,000 and then pays dividends to its shareholders totalling £100,000, its dividend cover is 3. In other words, the total dividends paid by the company are covered 3 times by available earnings – it had three times as much cash as was needed to pay those dividends. It is a useful guide to corporate health since it gives an idea of how much spare cash flow the company has.

There is probably more confusion about the term 'price earnings ratio' than any other investment statistic presented in the financial press. The P/E ratio is merely another guide to a company's financial position. It measures the number of years earnings bought at that share price.

It is calculated first by dividing profits available for distribution (i.e. profit after normal charges including corporation tax, payments to minority interests, preference dividends etc) by the number of ordinary shares issued. The resulting figure (earnings per share) is then divided into the share price to give the P/E ratio. If the shares are 100p and net earnings per share are 10p, the price/earnings ratio is 10.

An investment appraisal rule of thumb is, all other things being equal, the lower the P/E the more atttractive the share. The P/E tells you two things: firstly it is a measure of relatively how highly the company is regarded by other investors (the higher the P/E the more popular the share), secondly it shows how many years at present earnings it would take to get the share price paid back (assuming all earnings were distributed).

So a high P/E indicates a well thought of company and lower chances of a quick return, except of course that one reason the company is highly sought after as a general rule is that its earnings are growing fast, so the share price is recovered a lot more quickly than the ratio would indicate. Conversely the lower P/E looks attractive for quick returns but this might be because other investors have discovered the company's position is precarious or even deteriorating, which could mean no return at all.

Summing up, if the small investor takes a fancy to a company's shares which have an 11·5 per cent yield, the dividend is covered three times, and if it has a price/earnings ratio of 6, the chances are that he has discovered a potentially sound investment. So much so that it looks almost suspicious – why has nobody else spotted it?

Needless to say there are other things to consider before diving into the market. The main thing is that the investment statistics are historical in the sense that they relate to the company's trading in the previous year. An investor should take advice on the company's prospects in the current year. The broker will be pleased to check the background of a company, with particular attention to the chairman's report published soon after the declaration of the company's profit and dividend figures. In his report the chairman usually gives guidance to shareholders on prospects for the (by then) current financial year.

Assuming the company looks set to make more money, the potential investor in the shares can expect a higher dividend, greater cover for the dividend, and a lower P/E ratio. It is by looking forward in this way that an investor can comfort himself that he has a good return by way of dividend with the prospect of an even bigger return when the company announces its improved results.

Judging the market

Success on the stock exchange is governed by two factors: picking the right security to buy (one that will produce an adequate return either in dividends, capital appreciation, or both), and picking the right time to buy it. If the market is about to be hit by a tidal wave of gloom even the soundest company's shares will slide; if there is an expectation of rising interest rates gilts will become cheaper.

Having plodded through the selection process to pick the right security, the canny investor must then turn his mind to

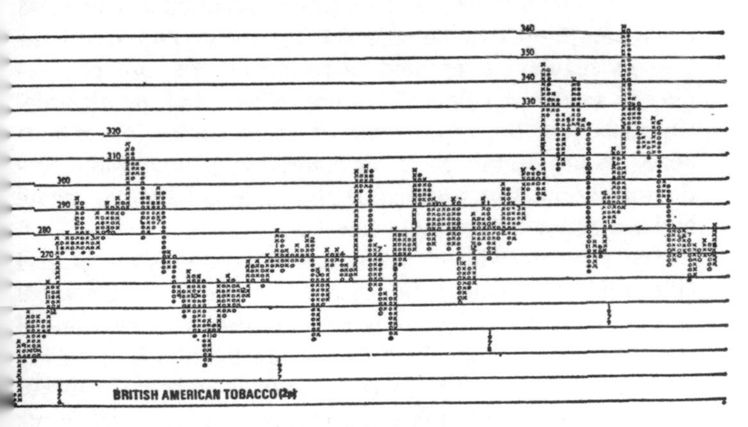

Chart by Chart Analysis

gauging market sentiment. This is essential not only for knowing when to buy but just as much for knowing when to sell. A mixture of instinct and economic awareness is needed but there are some techniques to help. The point about them is to think of them as tools for assessing the situation or as help in making up one's mind, not as signposts to be followed blindly.

Chartists

A wide range of techniques have been evolved to try to identify which share to buy and when. Roughly they can be divided into two main groups – those which look at an individual company and calculate its worth and prospects, and those which concentrate on the stock market itself. The former assumes fundamental value is a good investment and in any case will eventually be discovered by others; the latter says the only value of anything is what someone will pay for it.

The main technique of this second sort – 'technical analysis' – uses charts of share price movements. This is on the assumption that Stock Exchange behaviour moves in broadly regular or repeated patterns so if the start of a sequence becomes evident its later phases are predictable. Chartists plot the movements of share prices (or of gilt-edged securities, currencies or commodities) and make predictions about which direction the price is likely to move, and sometimes will even say how far.

The problem with charts is that interpreting the graphs still requires judgment. In other words, there is still a large degree of personal feeling in what purports to be a more scientific approach to share dealing. In the hands of an experienced and sensitive operator, charts can provide useful pointers. Their main interest, however, is a more circuitous one – a number of professional investors, such as financial institutions usually examine charts. Their buying and selling decisions may partly be affected by what they see. So an important factor is the effect charts have on these investors, and hence share prices.

Chartists plot both the overall market trend as reflected by the share indices and the movements in individual companies' shares. But since the process requires interpretative talent there is little firm evidence that following the passage of a chart can be any more successful in investment terms than, say, following the advice of a stockbroker or other market observer. The chartists have their place in the stock market scene by giving additional dimensions to share analysis but should be believed no more than other analysts.

Take-over bids

Take-over bids often hit the headlines because they involve large amounts of money and sometimes a battle. The buying company is trying to expand rapidly without the pain and expense of starting from scratch, and this is made all the more attractive if it can pick up a company cheaply. Even when the offer is substantially higher than the prevailing price of the shares, the directors of the company being bid for often pronounce it completely inadequate. Quite apart from pique and understandable worries about personal future employment, the board does this for the laudable reason of trying to get shareholders the best possible price.

Sometimes the bidder is forced to raise the price, and on occasion another suitor is flushed out into the open by the scrap. While this is going on shareholders in the target company will be enjoying a sudden strength in the share price – sometimes even higher than the last offer in the hope of better bids being on the way – and they can either sell at a handsome profit or hang on for developments.

This is probably another situation where the small investor lucky enough to hold shares in a company which becomes the subject of a take-over bid should avoid the temptation to be greedy. In a take-over battle there is always the chance that the bidding company will decide the price has become too high and decide to withdraw from the scene. If that happens the price of the take-over target would almost certainly fall back in the market. But like most investment decisions this is one of fine judgment, and no rules can be laid down. It has usually been right to hold on because the company's defence has more often than not forced an increased offer for the shares.

Take-over bidders often buy with the shares of their own companies rather than cash. In that case shareholders of the target company have three choices:

1 They can sell their existing shares in the market before the bid succeeds or fails
2 They can accept the shares in the bidding company and then sell those in the market
3 They can accept the shares in the bidding company and retain them as part of their investment holdings.

If the offer is in cash they merely have to decide whether to sell before the outcome is known and if they hang on, whether to accept the offer. Sometimes there is a share offer with a cash alternative and this is usually structured to make the shares seem a slightly better deal. But that decision will depend on one's view of the bidding company.

Rights and Scrip Issues

From time to time, investors will see announcements that companies are making 'rights' or 'scrip' issues. A rights issue is merely a means of a company raising new money for expansion, or to reduce its short-term borrowings at the bank by offering existing shareholders the right to buy more shares from the company, usually below the current price. If a company announces a rights issue of one-for-six at 80p per share when the shares are already quoted in the market standing at 100p, this means that an existing holder with, say, 600 shares, would be entitled to buy another 100 shares at 80p each. If the existing shareholder cannot afford to take up his rights he can, of course, sell them in the market.

Companies often issue new shares to existing holders for nothing. This is called a 'scrip' issue, and is merely a book-keeping exercise, often designed to improve the market-ability of shares. If a company is doing well, its share price in the Stock Exchange could get to quite a high level – say, 400p. This tends to discourage small investors who are irrationally put off by high-priced shares, because they get so few for their money. A company might, therefore, decide to make a 200 per cent scrip issue by issuing two new shares for every one held by existing shareholders. There is no immediate advantage in this because, while shareholders would end up with three times as many shares, the market quotation would be adjusted from 400p to 133p.

However, the chances are that the lower price could prompt wider interest in the shares, and that the market value would improve accordingly.

Capital gains tax

Money made from investment on the Stock Exchange is subject to capital gains tax. Several changes have been made in the system since it was first introduced and some of these have been intended to help and encourage the small investor who is slowly being crowded out of the stock market by the major institutions.

An investor can now make a profit on shares dealings of up to £5,300 without being liable to capital gains tax. Anything over that is taxed at the flat rate of 30%.

Losses on share transactions incurred during the financial year can be offset against profits in the same year and it is the resulting net figure on which capital gains tax is levied. If an individual has a net loss on share transactions during the financial year he can carry this loss forward to offset it against profit in the following year. But the losses brought forward will be used only to cover gains of over £1,000.

If you are confused by capital gains tax, remember you only need to start worrying when your share dealings are yielding a net profit of over £5,300. And if you are already showing a trading profit of over £5,300 why should you worry about anything.

INVESTMENT GUIDELINES

This book is mainly intended to describe the processes and procedures of the Stock Exchange and why things there happen the way they do. It is not primari[illegible] be an investment guide though inevitably refer[illegible]tedly been made to how investors can and sho[illegible]. But it might be helpful to pull out some of th[illegible]n the rest of the book and bring together a brie[illegible]nes to investing on the Stock Exchange.

- Do not buy shares unless you can [illegible]se that money. In other words, Stock Exchange [illegible] is only sensible after you have bought your ho[illegible]out life assurance, and have some rainy-day m[illegible] safely by. Emergency cash is not for shares since yo[illegible] be forced to sell on a depressed market.

- Unless you are a complete gambler do not put all your money into one share. It is uneconomic to scatter a small sum among a large number of securities so if you want to spread risks with your modest savings, consider investment and unit trusts.

- Pick your investment with care. Decide what it is you want in cold isolation before searching for the right company: income, capital growth, security, etc. Then you can go on to consider whether a 'blue chip' is suitable, or if you need a company with major export contracts and so on. Glamour industries like electronics (or whatever is this year's fashion) can be good but remember some companies will still founder while others prosper. Check yields, price/earnings ratios, and read the newspapers. Stockbrokers can also help. For the wealthier there are other sources such as merchant banks and portfolio investment companies. Extel Statistical Services, 37 Paul Street, London EC2, produces very useful cards of detailed information on every quoted company.

- In addition to ordinary shares there are fixed interest securities from companies like debentures and loan stocks, as well as government stocks (gilts) and local authority bonds.

- Wherever you put your money keep watching it. This is not to say you should bounce between exultation and gloom at each price movement, but only constant attention to both the company and the market as a whole can enable you to trade sensibly.

- And trading is what the stock market is about. Shares are not intended to be bought and then sealed in a vault for perpetuity. Sensible trading can yield far better returns than being locked into even sound shares.

- Be very wary of tips. Often they are mere 'ramps' carefully set up to boost prices for professional dealers; frequently they are wrong; even when they are right the price may well have been adjusted for the rumour long before you hear about it. For instance a newspaper tip will often provoke a flurry and hence higher prices – don't chase up the share for fear of losing a bargain. Wait a few days for the price to drift back and then you can act in a more sensible atmosphere. In any case check not only the truth of a tip but also its age.

- Remember the share price quoted in newspapers is the middle market price so you would buy at a higher and sell at a lower price, even if the market has not moved. And since the Stock Exchange is an open market with different rates being charged, there may be disagreement about what the average price is. So papers may print slightly different prices.

- Although the official Stock Exchange opening hours are 9.30 a.m. to 3.30 p.m. business can be done after the close. Broking and jobbing offices are usually manned until 5.30 p.m. and deals can be arranged over the phone.

- If a parcel of shares is bought and sold within the same fortnightly Stock Exchange 'account' the costs of trading are lower: there is only one broker's commission (for buying) and there is no government stamp duty.

- Don't be greedy. If a share becomes so fashionable its price soars beyond all sensible criteria, the time may well have come to sell since the reaction is likely to be just as violent. There is no point trying to get out right at the top or regretting the few percentage points foregone – nobody can hit it spot on except by luck.

- It is wasteful and expensive though to leap in and out of holdings at every movement. The trading expenses can quickly outweigh the gains. So think out your strategy in advance and work out what would make you switch holdings.

- Do not be afraid to cut a loss. If a share is sinking like a stone, hanging on in mere blind hope of improvement is a waste of money. Switching what is left of the money to a good investment is often a better policy.

- On the other hand do not panic at every down turn. If you know the company is sound, its prospects are good and your investment continues to yield a reasonable return it might be best to ignore the vagaries of stock market emotion. Share prices can be volatile both for individual companies and for the market as a whole and reacting to every gust of rumour can lose you money. Bear markets can easily stampede inexperienced investors (and often some who ought to know better) into unloading shares in sound companies only to find no better home for their cash and to see the market unexpectedly recover and leave them with a lost opportunity for profit.

Above all remember that stock market investments are not a sure way of making money but care, thought and some work can minimise the risks. Good luck.

STOCK EXCHANGE CAREERS

For the young man, or woman, interested in finance, the Stock Exchange can provide a really worth-while career. As I have already explained there are two types of firms operating on the Stock Exchange, jobbers and brokers. The schoolboy or girl who wants a career in the market has to consider whether he, or she, wants to work for a jobber, who has no direct dealings with the public, or for a broker, whose day-to-day business involves constant contact with investors. The member firms on the Stock Exchange show considerable variation in size. The larger firms may have 30 or 40 partners, backed by a staff of perhaps 500, while the opposite end of the scale would see perhaps a two-partner firm, with a staff of only six people.

If a school-leaver is prepared to start at the bottom with a view to learning the business, the usual way of making a start to a career is to apply for a post as a 'blue button'. Qualifications needed for this post are not particularly demanding, but an aptitude for figures, a lively mind, and a smart appearance are the basics for such a post. On the subject of smart appearance, the Stock Exchange has unwritten rules about dress, and member firms are unlikely to take on a 'blue button' who comes to a job interview in sweater and jeans, and perhaps long untidy hair.

Years ago, the Stock Exchange had a fairly rigid code of dress with men expected to wear a dark suit, a white shirt and a quiet tie. Members still wear fairly sober suits, but conditions have relaxed to the extent that somewhat more flamboyant shirts and ties have become acceptable.

Female workers in the Stock Exchange are expected to wear dresses or suits – slacks are frowned upon. Although these standards of dress may seem a little old fashioned, the Stock Exchange is one of the main financial centres of the world, and to maintain the investors' confidence it feels it cannot afford poor standards in appearance.

The boy or girl who was applying for the post of 'blue button' would be visualizing a career on the floor of the Stock Exchange but there are many other opportunities in normal office work in jobbers' and brokers' offices, covering computer operations, secretarial duties and the handling of paper work connected with share transactions.

A blue button's function is basically that of a market messenger in the sense that the job involves constant circulation on the market floor obtaining prices, and generally helping with the process of investment. This is an interesting job, and the blue button with a firm of jobbers will stand on the pitch with the more senior members of the firm, and take instructions from them.

A jobber often has 'limits' in his book. These are prices at which brokers are prepared to buy and sell shares if the market moves enough. A broker may leave a limit to buy a share at, say, 100p, at a time when the price is 102p. If the market slips back, the jobber would be able to offer the shares at 100p, and the 'limit' comes into operation. The jobber would, in these circumstances, tell his blue button to find the broker concerned and tell him the shares were available at 100p. The blue button is not allowed to deal and in this case is employed as the bearer of a message. The broker having received the message would then visit the jobber and the deal would be done.

The blue button attached to a firm of brokers is mainly employed doing the market rounds, constantly checking lists of prices for clients. Here again, the blue button is not allowed to deal and merely acts as bearer of information. The natural progression of a blue button's career is to that of an authorized dealer.

If the blue button learns the trade, he or she is promoted. The council of the Stock Exchange can authorise blue buttons to deal if they can satisfy a panel of senior dealers of having learnt properly the rules and conventions that regulate the way business is done in the market. Then he or she can transact business on behalf of the firm: carry out the buy and sell orders. The jobber's 'authorised dealer' stands on the firm's pitch and makes prices to brokers and can deal. The broker's authorised dealer will also be allowed to trade on behalf of investment clients.

After some years the authorised dealer may decide to become a member of the Stock Exchange. This would make little difference to the work being carried out in the market but would bring an entitlement to a say in the affairs of the Stock Exchange through voting rights and the ability to become a full member of the firm.

The Stock Exchange requires potential members to pass fairly stiff examinations. Assuming the candidate passes the examination and is elected to membership by the council, the first problem is the entry fee which currently stands at £1,000. But the jobbing or broking firm concerned may then take the member into partnership. Partners in Stock Exchange firms have ultimate responsibility for dealings with the investing public and this is not a privilege and responsibility awarded lightly. Unlike blue buttons, authorised dealers and members who receive a basic salary plus a bonus (when the firm is doing well enough to afford it), a partner has a share in the profits (and losses) of the firm.

At this stage it is only fair to introduce a note of warning. During periods when overall business in the market falls to a low level, member firms are liable to find themselves with the normal heavy overheads but insufficient earnings to keep them profitable. In these circumstances stockbroking and jobbing firms are sometimes forced to make staff reductions. It must be recognized therefore that if business is bad in the stock market for a fairly long period then jobs can be at risk. Happily this does not happen very often.

Any young men or women thinking about a career on the Stock Exchange should write to the Information Department, The London Stock Exchange, Throgmorton Street, London EC2. This department is most helpful with advice and might even forward job applications to the Stock Exchange's own internal employment bureau to which firms notify their requirements. People outside London can find careers in the provincial exchanges around the country.

STOCK EXCHANGE PRICE INDICES

References to movements of Stock Exchange prices usually mention 'The Index'. In newspapers, on radio and television, the standard by which the fluctuations of the stock market is gauged is the Index. In fact there are several indices but the one usually referred to is the *Financial Times* Industrial Ordinary Index. This was first compiled in 1935 by the *Financial News* (which was subsequently merged into the *Financial Times*) and contains the shares of 30 leading companies spread across many of the main industrial activities. When first compiled the Index contained

Associated Portland Cement
Austin Motors
Bass
Bolsover Colliery
Callenders Cables
J. & P. Coats
Courtaulds
Distillers
Dorman Long
Dunlop Rubber
Electric and Musical Industries
Fine Spinners
General Electric
Guest Keen & Nettlefolds
Harrods
Hawker Siddeley
Imperial Chemical Industries
Imperial Tobacco
International Tea
London Brick
Murex
Patons and Baldwins
Pinchin Johnson
Rolls-Royce
Tate and Lyle
Turner & Newall
United Steel
Vickers
Watney Combe and Reid
F. W. Woolworth

Austin Motors' successor, British Leyland, was finally removed only 40 years later in April 1975; Murex is now part of BOC International which is an Index stock; Watneys was taken over by Grand Metropolitan which has been in the Index since 1971; Pinchin Johnson was bought by Courtaulds, another Index stock; Bolsover Colliery, Dorman Long, United Steel, British Leyland and the aero engine division of Rolls-Royce have been nationalized; Associated Portland Cement has changed its name to Blue Circle Industries, Electric and Musical Industries was taken over by Thorn, and Imperial Tobacco became Imperial Group as it diversified.

Despite this degree of coming and going over more than 40 years, there is a degree of continuity so that the present list of 30 still has 10 of the original members (marked *).

Allied Lyons
Associated Dairies
Beecham Group
BICC
Blue Circle Industries
BOC International
Boots
Bowater
British Petroleum
BTR Industries
Cadbury Schweppes
Courtaulds*
Distillers*
Dunlop*
General Electric
Glaxo Group
Grand Metropolitan
Guest Keen and Nettlefolds*
Hawker Siddeley Group*
Imperial Chemical Industries*
Imperial Group*
London Brick*
Lucas Industries
Marks and Spencer
P & O Steam Navigation
Plessey
Tate + Lyle*
Thorn EMI
TI Group
Vickers*

The aim now, as it has been from the outset, is to pick leaders in a spread of industrial activities. The range gives breadth to the index and the size of the constituent companies provides a substantial slice of the industrial market.

The main purpose of the 30 share index (or just *FT* Index as it is called) is to provide an up-to-the-minute indication of the temper of the Stock Exchange. With its concentration on only 30 shares it is more volatile than indices which cover a larger number of shares and so reflects more sensitively the swings of market sentiment. But since they are leading British companies, the movements are taken to be a fair reflection of the way investors view the stock market in general as well as, by implication, their feelings about the UK economy.

The Index is calculated hourly from 10 a.m., half an hour after the market opens, to 3 p.m., and there is a final closing price for the day collected from the jobbers' offices after trading has finished, at 5 p.m. (Official trading stops at 3.30 p.m. but there is often some 'after hours' business done over the telephone as traders clear their books.)

The calculation of the Index sounds terrifyingly complicated but was in fact evolved precisely because it was easier to produce figures this way in practice than by any of the suggested alternatives. The Index is the geometric mean of each share's price, divided by the price at the base date. This calculation is done by adding the logarithms of the share values, deducting the base value, dividing by 30, and then taking the antilog of the result.

Difficult as that sounds, the working out can be done in minutes which was important in 1935 when electronic calculators were not available to enable people to produce more sophisticated Index analyses. The geometric mean is used to allow for the fact that the actual cash prices of shares are very different. A rise of 3p in a share costing 600p is not nearly as significant as in one costing 30p, and if the index did not reflect this it would provide very misleading information about the degree of market movement. Another reason is that a simple average (arithmetic mean) produces curious results. If there are two shares costing 100p each, and the price of one doubles whilst the other halves, the average would be $\frac{200+50}{2} = 125$. This would clearly be misleading and the geometric mean has the advantage of producing an index that remains at 100.

There are still some problems with the Index as it is, one of which is that it has a downward bias of about 0·8 per cent a year. But the Index is now so well established and its shortcomings are so minor that they are not reckoned to be bad enough to warrant the upheaval of a major change.

For more sophisticated calculations of how the market has moved or to see how various sectors are faring, there is a large number of other indicators. There are nearly 50 indices for equities sectors, plus 14 for gilt-edged securities, and another 3 for industrial fixed interest issues, with all these indices being based on over 750 securities. These are the *Financial Times* Actuaries Indices, so called because they were evolved with and are supervised by the Institute of Actuaries. They cover a wide range of industrial groups such as Food Manufacturing, Breweries, Chemicals, Merchant Banks, Insurance Brokers, Heavy Engineering, etc.

These industry indices are then grouped to provide indices for related branches of industries such as Durable Consumer Goods, Capital Goods and so on. Finally they are amalgamated further to provide the Industrial Group which covers 496 shares, the 500 Share Index (which is really the Industrial Group plus four oil company shares), and the All Share Index covering 651 companies. Clearly the All Share Index does not cover all quoted companies but it is reckoned to include all the significant ones, and so will provide a fair guide to the movement of the market as a whole.

Since these indices weight each company's price by the total value of the shares on issue, they reflect general conditions and can be adjusted for inflation to see how the values have moved in real terms. Trying to do this for the *FT* Industrial Ordinary Index produces misleading results. At the end of 1977 for instance the Index stood at 485·4 and if this is adjusted for inflation it comes out as 52·24 – about the level the Index stood at in real terms in the autumn of 1932. But this depressing result does not truly represent the value because it does not fully allow for script issues by the Index companies, and because it still includes that 0·8 per cent annual downward bias. All the same, it does show the disastrous effects of inflation on investments.

THE UNLISTED SECURITIES MARKET

In November 1980 the Stock Exchange started a new market for companies too small or too young to qualify for a full quotation, or for companies whose directors were unwilling to release the 25% of the equity normally required. Since they were not granted full market quotation, it was called the Unlisted Securities Market (USM).

Before this market was started, dealings could take place in unlisted companies under a special Stock Exchange rule (Rule 163(2)) but this was allowed only under strict supervision, with every bargain needing Stock Exchange approval: any proposed deal had to be recorded on a special form and checked by the exchange before the transaction was confirmed.

Rule 163 (2) remains and deals can still be done by this means but the Stock Exchange has reserved this facility for shares dealt very occasionally.

The aim of the USM is to give smaller companies access to the dealing facilities of the market and to give them greater flexibility for raising additional finance by share or loan capital. In return they do have to accept some Stock Exchange regulation and must disclose extensive financial and other information, but need not go through the expensive process of a full listing.

A company seeking a USM quotation must be registered as a public limited company under the Companies Acts and it must normally have been trading for at least three years. Exceptions can be made to the minimum trading period – for example where the future is sufficiently clear to justify firm forecasts, or for new high technology companies without a track record.

The Stock Exchange has also set procedural requirements for entry to the USM:

1 The public must be offered at least 10% of the issued ordinary capital (companies with a full listing must have at least 25% in outside hands).

2 The shares are normally marketed by a *placing*. In a placing a sponsor organisation buys the shares to be issued from the company and then places them (i.e. sells them), at a slightly higher price, with clients of its own choosing. But the sponsor must reserve a quarter of the issue for offering to the jobbers who will be dealing in these shares.

Though placing is normal other methods of launching a USM company are also permitted.

An *offer for sale* is arranged through a stockbroker who offers the shares for sale to the public at a fixed price. In an *offer for sale by tender* the price is not fixed and investors are invited to tender for shares at a price they decide, above a fixed minimum. *Introduction* is the cheapest entry to the USM and is for companies which already have around 10% of their capital in public hands. In contrast with the other methods an introduction requires no additional capital to be issued since no shares are being offered and is used by companies whose shares have already been regularly traded under existing Stock Exchange special rules.

3 All companies applying for a quotation on the USM are

required to provide particulars for the Exchange Telegraph (Extel) USM service.
4 All companies entering the USM must sign the General Undertaking of the Stock Exchange, promising continuing disclosure of information to enable the investing public to monitor the state of the company.
5 Conditions of USM entry do not require formal advertising of a full prospectus or other statistical information in a daily newspaper (as they would for full listing) but the event must be recorded with a "box advertisement" in at least one leading newspaper, with abridged details, including reference to the availability of the Extel card new issues card.

Although Stock Exchange supervision of the USM is less comprehensive than of fully listed company markets, there is monitoring and protection for the investor. The USM is covered by the Stock Exchange compensation fund in the same way as for listed companies.

A goodly number of small companies have already taken advantage of the USM to secure quotation for their shares, and the odds are that this sector will grow in size and interest over the years.

The Author

Norman Whetnall has been stock market editor for the *The Daily Telegraph* City pages for the past twenty years. Before that he worked for the *Financial Times*. He has also contributed to a number of journals in Britain and Canada.

He is married and has two daughters, a son and a beagle.

Acknowledgments

In expressing my sincere thanks for all the help and encouragement provided by friends and associates in the London Stock Exchange, I would particularly like to mention Alan Westmarland of stockbrokers, De Zoete & Bevan, whose expertise in the gilt-edged market made a complicated subject relatively easy to understand. Also special thanks to my colleague on *The Daily Telegraph*, Michael Becket, whose comments and suggestions on the early text contributed much to the end result.

Norman Whetnall.

Other publications from Flame Books

Big Business and Government: the new disorder – Neville Abraham

A highly-acclaimed analysis of the complex relations between all large organisations (both nationalised and private sector) and the politicians and their civil servants. Mr Abraham also has some highly controversial suggestions on how the problems might be overcome.

The press and distinguished public figures gave the book an overwhelming reception on its appearance. Here are examples:

Lord Robens said it 'has opened the doors on the corridors of Whitehall and enables us to see at close range the problems that we face', and called it 'a "must" reading for those who want to see progressively increasing higher standards of living'.

Sir Richard Marsh said 'Neville Abraham's book makes a major contribution to the discussion and has the additional virtue of being highly readable'.

The Economist commented that 'he brings to his writing the objectivity, intelligence and realism of the best kind of civil servant'.

Professor Grigor McClelland thought the book 'informative, up-to-date, clear and readable', adding that 'it becomes ever more necessary to understand the topics with which Mr Abraham deals and it would be difficult to find a better guide to them'.

ISBN 0 905340 01 9 334 pages £3.40

Investor Power: a guide to shareholder rights – Barbara Conway

Investors often see their companies founder when early action might have saved their hard-won savings. This brief, down-to-earth guide shows how to spot approaching problems and what shareholders can do to stop the rot. In simple language it explains what the company's accounts actually tell you, what to look out for, and how to act. The advice ranges from how to use the financial Press to when to notify the Fraud Squad; how to call an extraordinary general meeting and where information is available.

ISBN 0 905340 03 5 £1.35

Economic Alphabet – Michael Becket

Such was the success of the first edition of this irreverent but informative look at what lies behind the jargon of the headlines, that a second enlarged edition has been hurriedly prepared. Economics and the stock exchange seem permanently to be in the news but the vocabulary gets ever more complex. What is the International Monetary Fund or the EMS (European Monetary System); what happens when a currency floats; who are the monetarists and why; is base rate the same as minimum lending rate? All this and very much more is simply explained.

ISBN 0 905340 04 3 £1.85

Value for Money Insurance: what to buy and how to buy it

There is such an enormous range of insurance policies that bewildered consumers cannot know what is available, much less decide what is the best buy. To help them ask the right questions and buy all the cover they need (and no more) a plain-language guidebook has been sponsored by the British Insurance Brokers' Association.

Written by experts in each of the areas covered, the book discusses almost any policy an individual is likely to need: home contents, house structure, car, health, life, holidays, pension; and even the less usual ones like insurance against having twins or the village fete being washed out by a storm. There is also an introduction to business insurance and professional indemnity.

ISBN 0 0905340 06 X £2.95

If you have any difficulty obtaining any of these books, want to know more about them or about future publications, write to
Flame Books Ltd
9 Kensington Park Gardens
London W11